Run, Rabbit, Run

The Hilarious and Mostly True Tales of Rabbit Maranville

Walter "Rabbit" Maranville
Introduction by Harold Seymour, Ph.D.
Afterword by Bob Carroll

D1264380

SOCIETY FOR AMERICAN BASEBALL RESEARCH
Cleveland, Ohio

Copyright 1991, Society for American Baseball Research, Inc.
"Who Was Rabbit Maranville?" copyright 1991, Robert Carroll
Introduction copyright 1991, Harold Seymour, Ph.D.

All rights reserved. No part of this book may be reproduced or transmitted
in whole or in part in any form or by any means, electronic or mechanical,
including photocopying, recording, or by any information storage or re-
trieval system, without permission in writing by the
Society for American Baseball Research, Inc.,
P.O. Box 93183, Cleveland, Ohio 44101.

Production by Baseball Ink
Design by The Knickerbocker Design Group

Printed in the United States of America.

First printing: March 1991.

ISBN 0-910137-44-7

Contents

Acknowledgments

There were many people who labored to make this book a reality. Thanks must go to: Ralph and Dallas Graber for salvaging Rabbit Maranville's autobiography from dusty solitude; Paul Adomites, SABR's former Publications Director, for his early efforts to bring this manuscript to light; Alan McKnight and The Knickerbocker Design Group for their design talents; and Michael Schacht, for the cover painting and interior silhouettes.

Also, Mark Rucker; Pat Kelly of the National Baseball Library; Mike Saporito; Atlantic Typesetting, of Latham, New York, for their typesetting expertise; Mueller & Jadatz, of Albany, New York, for providing color separations; and printer EBSCO Media, of Birmingham, Alabama.

Lastly, for their guidance and assistance throughout the production of this book, thanks must go to A.D. Suehsdorf and the SABR Publications Committee.

Introduction

When I recall Rabbit Maraville I see him at Ebbets Field sneaking up behind an umpire who was arguing with one of Rabbit's teammates. Rabbit drops down on all fours behind him and then, grinning, motions to the player to shove the umpire so that when the arbiter falls he'll go heels over head. Fans in the park are enjoying the episode, as does the player who is arguing.

That was Rabbit, a small, thin, wiry guy. Although possessing only an ordinary arm, Maranville was a very good ballplayer. He was also tough, strong, and belligerent, but never lacking in ideas for practical jokes. Once I saw him protest against an umpire's calling a very low ball a strike by dropping to his knees and making a few practice swipes with his bat. I enjoyed watching him play when he came to Ebbets Field, where I was a batboy for visiting teams two summers in the twenties. Then I saw him at even closer quarters when he joined the Dodgers the year I got promoted to serve as batboy for the Robins themselves, under Wilbert Robinson, known as Uncle Robbie. Many times I watched Maranville make what was known in Brooklyn as his "basket catch," in which he centered himself carefully under a high fly ball and caught it low at his belt line, using the ordinary "pancake" glove common in those early days.

One would think Rabbit the last person to write up these incidents, but he did, and they ring true. His escapades vary from the amusing to the hilarious. My favorites are the story about the way he recovered his wife's jewels from beneath the skirt of a subway passenger and another about fooling pitcher Jack Scott into thinking Scott had choked him to death. Readers will select their own favorites—there are plenty to go around. Rabbit also contributes something serious to baseball history: a new slant on the Merkle play.

John Holway has expertly shaped these stories , editing out, with a very light tough, a few extraneous details so that the main point of each tale shines through. Bob Carroll has added an afterword explaining, to those of you who know little about Rabbit, how good (and how colorful) his career really was.

Now sit back and enjoy yourself.

HAROLD SEYMOUR, PH.D.

Editor's Notes

Rabbit Maranville was the Joe Garagiola of Grandpa's day. Or maybe he was the Jay Johnstone. In a twenty-four-year career from 1912 through 1936, Rabbit found a lot of funny situations to laugh at. No wonder. He caused most of them himself.

Few fans alive today have had the privilege of sitting down for a few beers with the Rabbit and listening to him spin his tales. But fortunately for us, a year before his death in 1954, Rabbit reached back forty years into his memory and put his stories down on paper after the urging of his daughter and Max Kase, former sports editor of the New York *Journal-American*, who had employed Maranville in a public relations position. Unfortunately, Maranville did not finish his autobiography before he died. For decades the tales rested, virtually unread, until the Graber brothers, Dallas and Ralph, discovered the manuscript inconspicuously offered for sale by a memorabilia dealer and bought it rescuing it for all future fans to enjoy.

The stories give us much autobiographical material about Rabbit. But they are not an autobiography, any more than *Baseball Is a Funny Game* is the autobiography of Garagiola. They tell us much history. And yet they do not comprise a history, any more than *Veeck as in Wreck* is a history of the Cleveland Indians.

Rabbit's memory played tricks on him, not surprising to anyone who has interviewed old men reaching back into the past. Where errors were found, I have attempted to correct them. Where Rabbit's somewhat Lardneresque prose has breached some rules preached in sixth-grade English classes, I did my best to make him readable without making him slick. In short, I tried to let Rabbit be Rabbit.

To fill in the details of Rabbit's life not covered in his stories, Bob Carroll has delved into the records and penned a more scholarly account of dates, places, and names in Bob's own irreverent, even Maranvillian, style.

So I invite you to join us at the beer house after a SABR meeting, pull up a chair next to the popcorn bowl, and share the company of our madcap guide, who will open doors into a world few of us never knew.

JOHN HOLWAY
JANUARY 1991

Run, Rabbit, Run

The Rabbit cultivated eccentricity into an art form. His brain followed the direction of his cap, most definitely askew.

Rabbit Runs for His Life

While training in Hot Springs when I was with the Pittsburgh Pirates, we stayed at the Eastman Hotel. Hot Springs is a dead town when night comes. Almost all of the streets are dead-end streets as they all run into the mountains. I was sitting in the lobby one evening when one of our players came up to me and said, "There is a beautiful girl, Rabbit. Have you seen her around the lobby?"

I said, "Yes, I have, and she really is nice."

He said, "Would you like to meet her?"

I said, "Stop your kidding; you never met that girl." He said he had and that he would make a date for me. I said, "It's okay with me."

My fellow ballplayer came up to me a couple of days later and said, "I made the date for you for the following night up at her apartment."

I said, "Okay with me."

My friend said to me when I told him okay that the girl was married, that her husband was a conductor on the railroad. He also said, "Get some fruit and a dozen bottles of beer, and I'm sure you will have a very nice social evening with her."

I said, "It's okay with me."

The next day, around five o'clock in the afternoon I met my teammate and he said to me, "Rabbit, let's take a walk down to the train and see if her husband is working tonight." We went down to the station and at five-thirty PM the conductor yelled, "All aboard." My good friend ballplayer said, "That's him, Rabbit; you are set for tonight." I went out and bought a basket of fruit and a dozen bottles of beer.

My date was at nine o'clock, and it was only a few streets away from the hotel. I went up to the address given me, which was an apartment building. I opened the front door and walked along the dark corridor looking for the suite number when out of the darkness came two pistol shots and a voice yelling at me, "So you're the guy that's trying to steal my wife away from me. I'll kill you." He took a couple of more shots in the meantime.

When I heard the shots and his voice, beer went one way and the fruit another and I ran for the door, ran out to the middle of the street as fast as my legs could take me. I think everyone in town knew of the frame-up, for the faster I ran, the crowd lined up on each side of the street kept yelling, "Run, kid, run." While I was running to get away from the crazy husband, my eyes spotted the Government Hotel in front of me and, running as hard as I could, I streaked through the lobby down to the men's room, jumped into a pay toilet, and sat there.

I sat there about two hours and hearing no noise about, I left my hiding place and went back to our hotel. I put two and two together that night in bed and decided that it was a frame-up and that my teammate never knew the girl at all... also that I never saw a train pull out of a station without a conductor aboard.

Getting His Nickname

Most people know me by the name of Rabbit. If you asked them my real name, they couldn't tell you. Well, it's Walter James for you who don't know. I was playing for New Bedford, Massachusetts (known as the Whalers) in the old New England League in 1912. I was very friendly with a family by the name of Harrington. They were real baseball fans. Mr. and Mrs. Harrington had five daughters and one son. They all worked in the shoe factory except one little daughter seven years old and the old gent who was a coal driver. One night I was down to their house having dinner with them when Margaret, the second oldest daughter, asked me if I could get two passes for the next day's game, as she wanted to take her seven-year-old sister to see me play.

I said, "Sure, I'll leave them in your name at the Press Gate."

She said, "And come down to dinner after the game."

I left the two passes as I promised and after the game I went down to their house for dinner. I rang the door bell and Margaret came and opened the door and said, "Hello, Rabbit."

I said, "Where do you get that Rabbit stuff?"

She said, "My little seven-year-old-sister (Skeeter) named you that because you hop and bound around like one."

The name Rabbit still sticks with me after all of these years, and I hope it will until that Great Umpire says, "It's time for you, Rabbit, to get in your hole."

Up to the Majors

In the year of 1912, while I was playing for the New Bedford club in the New England League, I was sold to the Boston Braves for $1,000 (cash). I was told to report to Johnny Kling, manager of the Boston club, in the fall.

I reported to the Boston club on September 4, 1912. I was given a uniform of one of the pitchers on the club by the name of Ed Donnelly. He was 6' 1" tall and seemed to weigh 250 pounds. You can imagine how I looked in a uniform of that size. However, I managed to make myself look presentable after taking many rolls in the pants. After looking over my fellow players hitting and the size of them, I didn't feel any too confident of making the big league. I looked around the park, and in the outfield playing right field I spotted a little short fellow like myself wearing a mustache. My confidence was quickly restored in making good in the big time. I said to myself, "What is this, an old man's league, or is somebody kidding me?" After I saw him hit, I changed my mind as he was one of the best hitters in baseball. He chewed tobacco and always had a toothpick that he held on the right side of his mouth. They called him, as I found out later, Toothpick John Titus.

The first club I played against was the old Chicago Cubs under the management of Frank Chance. You folks can understand what a ribbing I took weighing 126 pounds to those big brutes, Harry Steinfeldt 3B, Joe Tinker SS, Johnny Evers 2B, Frank Chance lB, Jimmy Archer C, Ed Reulbach P, Jimmy Sheckard LF, Tommy Leach CF, Frank Schulte RF. I gave back everything they called me by just saying, "Wait until I grow up and I'll take care of you," which I did in years to come.

The fall of 1912 my fielding was above the average. My hitting was not so good. However, I was the talk of the town because of my peculiar way of catching a fly ball. They later named it the Vest-pocket Catch. Boston wasn't drawing any too good, but it seemed like everyone that came out to the park came to see me make my peculiar catch or get hit on the head. [Maranville caught popups at his belt buckle, just as Willie Mays did. The ball almost "grazed his uniform," says A. D. Suehsdorf, who saw him do it.] Many of the players passed different remarks about my catch which wouldn't go in print. I do, however, remember what Jimmie Sheckard said: "I'll bet you he don't drop three fly balls in his career, no matter how long or short he may be in the game." They asked him why he said that. He said, "Notice the Kid is perfectly still, directly under the ball, and in no way is there any vibration to make the ball bounce out of his glove."

The last day of that fall season I was talking to one of our pitchers by the name of Hub Perdue. He was called the Gallatin Squash on account of his shape. He came from Gallatin, Tennessee. In his southern dialect, which I could hardly understand, I listened to his advice for next year. He said, "Rabbit, I like you and all the players like you and the people of Boston love you. I don't know what you are getting in salary, but if you don't get yourself $3,000 next year, don't talk to me." I thanked him for his advice and we went on our different ways. I received my contract for 1913, which was for $1,800. I thought of what Hub Perdue told me and I immediately sent it back and told them I couldn't sign for that as I had decided baseball wasn't for me.

The following week I received a contract for $2,400, which to me looked like a fortune. I signed at once and sent it back to Boston.

Opening at Shortstop

In 1913 we trained in Athens, Georgia, a little college town, and we worked out on the college grounds.

George (Tweedy) Stallings, who came from Haddock, Georgia, took over the Boston club. He was in my opinion one of the greatest managers in baseball. He was also a great builder of character in men. Baseball needed men of his character and learning, as most of the players in those days came right off of the farm. One day in the hotel we were staying at, some of the boys were waiting for their breakfast order. As they were getting more nervous for their food to come, [they] started throwing rolls and pieces of lump sugar. The minute they started throwing, the rest of the tables took it up and it got to be a regular ducking party. The throwing was at its highest when Stallings walked in to have his breakfast. He went to his table, looked around the dining room, but never said a word. The minute the players saw him, they stopped their throwing. That morning at the ballpark, as he was having his meeting on the day's work, he said, "Gentlemen, a man is considered a gentleman or a rowdy in accordance of how he behaves himself in a dining room."

The 1913 season started out for me at spring training like a hectic year. I had a feeling things were not going to be so good for the Rabbit, as I just couldn't get Stallings settled in my mind.

In 1913 I had as my opponent a boy named Art Bues, who came up from Buffalo. He was Stallings' nephew. Coming from the park after our afternoon session, I was walking with a big first baseman by the name of Gus Metz. He said, "Rabbit, did you see where they have the ballclub picked?"

I said, "No, who have they decided on for shortstop?"

He said, "Art Bues, Stallings' nephew." I was as mad as a hatter. I said, "If I couldn't play ball better than that guy I'd quit." Walking behind us was Stallings, and he overheard what I said unbeknown to us. That evening after dinner I was loafing around the lobby of the hotel when Stallings came along and said, "I want to talk to you."

I said, "Okay." We went over to a sofa and sat down (I'm still burning up).

Stallings said, "You don't like my selection of Bues for shortstop over you."

I said, "No, I don't."

"Well," Mr. Stallings said, "You have a lot to learn and I'm running this club and I'll make my own selections no matter what you or anybody else thinks."

I said, "That's okay with me; I'm not trying to run your ballclub but if I'm not a better ballplayer than that relative of yours, I'll quit."

He said, "No, you will not; I'll keep you until we get back to Boston, then use you in a trade if I have the opportunity."

I didn't play any more shortstop for a couple of weeks, but I kept myself in good shape. We arrived in Atlanta, Georgia, on Easter Sunday. As I am a great believer in prayer, I went to church and received Holy Communion. That afternoon I got dressed in our room, as we always dressed at the hotel, and then got in a bus which took us to the ballpark. Going up Peach Tree Boulevard on our way to the park, a player who I don't remember right off hand told me I was to play shortstop that afternoon as Bues came down with a sore throat. We left Bues in Atlanta as he was a very sick boy and came into New York to open the season with the Giants.

Game time came along and Stallings yelled down the bench at me. "Rabbit, you're playing shortstop today."

I said, "Yes, and you will never get me out of there."

We faced Christy Mathewson that Opening Day against Hub Perdue. We beat Mathewson 8–3, and I did myself proud. I got three hits and fielded okay. Twenty-three years later I got out of playing shortstop, as I will tell you about later.

My first real bawling-out came in the year of 1913. It was the tenth inning of the game and we had the last time at bat as we were the home club. Our first man up, Hap Myers, singled to center field. I was given instructions to bunt him down to second base. The pitcher's first two tosses to me were balls. I tried to bunt the next one and fouled it off. The next pitch was a ball, which gave me the advantage on the pitcher. The count on me was 3-and-1. I tried to bunt the 3-and-1 pitch and popped up a little fly which the catcher caught. When I did that, you would think all hell broke loose. Stallings called me dumb, stupid no brain weasel. Everyone in the ballpark could hear him. I came back to the bench as mad as he was. I said, "What's the matter with you, you Big Pig? You told me to bunt and I tried and failed. What you squawking about?"

"Squawking!" he said. "You Dumb Dora, there was only one play to make and that was to take the ball and if it was a strike you still had the pitcher 3-and-2 and it would be a regular hit and run play."

I said, "Okay, I know the play now and it will never happen again." I have seen similar plays at the present day by Phil Rizzuto and Jerry Coleman, and I told them after the game about the bawling-out I got for doing the same thing. I never did try to bunt the 3-and-1 again in my baseball career.

The only thing of importance that happened in 1913 was that the

Braves finished out of last place. [Here, in another hand, was added, "On November 11, 1913, I was married to Elizabeth Shea of Chicopee Falls, Massachusetts."]

The Miracle Braves

Unbeknown to me and I guess the followers of baseball, 1914 was to be a wonderful year for baseball. The Braves made different trades that winter which turned out very good at the end of the season. During the winter the Boston club also purchased Johnny Evers from the Chicago Cubs for $25,000. Boston was full of excitement when they received the news. They loved Evers for his fighting spirit and especially his continuous arguments against umpires as to rules.

Evers and I worked at second and short like a charm. It was just Death Valley, whoever hit a ball down our way. Evers with his brains taught me more baseball than I ever dreamed about. He was psychic. He could sense where a player was going to hit if the pitcher threw the ball where he was supposed to.

We trained at Macon, Georgia, in the spring of 1914, and it was an ideal spot to train. Hot in the daytime and cool at night.

The season was on and we had made one swing around the eastern part of the schedule. We'd done the best we thought we could, but somehow we always came out on the losing end. We then made our first western trip. The impression we left was very bad considering we were a big league ballclub, When we got back east they started calling us Misfits, Country Buttered Ball Tossers, and what not. With all this Stallings, our manager, kept encouraging us by saying, "Stick in there; we will show them."

"Can You Play Better Ball?"

We continued to lose ballgame after ballgame with a win now and then. We were in the eyes of everyone just a bunch of misfits. However, Mr. James E. Gaffney, our owner and President of the club, thought different. He called us individually down to his office and signed us to our 1915 contracts. I was tickled to pieces to have a job for the following year.

On July 7 we were still in last place and we were to start on our last western trip. We had an off-day, but our secretary booked an exhibition game up in Buffalo, New York. Buffalo was in the International League and we were supposed to be the big leaguers, but Buffalo beat us, 12–3.

On our way to Chicago, Stallings was about to retire to his stateroom when he turned around and looked us all over. "Big leaguers," he said, "Baa! You couldn't even beat a bunch of females." After that little dynamic speech he closed the stateroom door with a slam bang. His speech left us all in a very angry mood.

Posies for the Rabbit from his Boston admirers. Johnny Evers won the MVP Award in the Miracle Year of 1914, but Maranville covered short as no one ever had before—and batted cleanup besides.

I finally broke the silence and said to Johnny Evers, "Can you play better ball than you have been playing?"

He said, "Yes, I think I can."

I said, "I think I can, too."

We asked everyone on the club, and they all said the same thing. We all jumped into our berths and called it a day. We arrived in Chicago the next morning for a four-game series with them. We defeated them three out of four games.

We then moved to St. Louis, who was only half a game back of the Giants. Every paper in town had in three-inch headlines, CARDINALS WILL BE IN FIRST PLACE WHEN LOWLY BRAVES LEAVE TOWN. We defeated the Cardinals two out of three games. We then went on to Cincinnati for four games. We defeated them three out of the four games we played them. We then went to Pittsburgh, where we opened up a five-game series and we defeated them four out of five games [all by shut-outs]. We then went on to win sixteen out of our next nineteen ball-games. From misfits we became the talk of the baseball world. What has got into those Braves? Everywhere we went we drew great crowds, and people said they would rather see the practice we put up before the game than the game itself.

Evers Teaches Rabbit a Lesson

My second bawling-out came from Johnny Evers in Boston. We were playing against the Cincinnati Red Legs. It was along in the eighth inning when Cincinnati had Tommy Clarke (catcher) on first base and a boy by the name of Martin Berghammer (a third baseman) on third. There was one out at the time. The batter hit the ball on the ground to Evers, who grabbed it up, and threw it to me. I was just about to throw it to first when Tommy Clarke came charging into me. I tried to throw around him so as not to harm him, and my throw to first base was not in time to get the runner and the run scored, which turned out to be the winning run. My delay in trying to throw around Clarke let out a blast of curses I have never heard since for not letting Clarke have it between the eyes. I said to Evers after his ballyhoo, "What should I have done?" I told him I didn't want to hurt Clarke.

He said, "You big sissy, the next time anyone comes down at you to stop a double play hit him between the eyes."

I said, "Okay, boy, I'll bust them all over."

About a month later we were playing in Cincinnati and the same condition prevailed. Clarke yelled down to me, "Give me plenty of room or I'll give you what I gave you in Boston." I never said a word but thought of what Evers told me to do. The ball was again hit to Evers and he threw it to me and Clarke came charging at me. There was no throwing around him this time. I hit him in the forehead between the eyes and the ball skidded off his nut into right field. Clarke laid as if dead at my feet and the run had scored from third which again turned out to be the winning run. All the players ran out to see how bad Clarke was injured, but he was coming around then to his senses. He said, "Well, you got me." Evers then came over and said to me, "That's the way to give it to them, Rabbit; they won't come down charging at you anymore."

A Hangover and a Headache

The year 1914 was a great one for me. Two incidents happened that I never will forget.

One I realize was an escapade, not an incident. Hank Gowdy, our catcher, had a friend of his by the name of Harry Levine. He was an importer of selective wines from France. Mr. Levine invited Hank to get some of the boys and come out to his house (in Hyde Park, Massachusetts) and have dinner and talk baseball. The whole family were great baseball fans. Hank got together for the party Josh Devore OF, Butch Schmidt 1B, Bill James P, Gene Cocreham P, Bert Whaling C, and myself.

We were introduced to the family—the Mrs., their son, and their daughter. We were invited to have a drink, which we did. Most of the players drank beer in those days. No hard stuff at all. We walked around his place, which was an estate, and it was beautiful. We were called that dinner was being served. We made a wild rush for the dining room. (I don't know if you ever gave a dinner to a bunch of ballplayers, but my advice to you is "Don't." I gave a dinner to a bunch of Pittsburgh ballplayers and served lamb. Cotton Tierney and Charlie Grimm wound up fighting over the bone.) We had a delicious dinner, and Mrs. Levine said, "Boys, if you will take a walk around the grounds, I'll have the dining room all cleared away so you can talk baseball. We walked around his estate for about an hour; then we headed back to the house and the dining room.

Gowdy, knowing the family, said to Mr. Levine, "Harry, let's have a drink." The start was made and the boys all got off even. I will never forget Mrs. Levine saying to me and Butch Schmidt, "You two stay on beer," and we promised her we would. Butch sat right next to me, and as the party got more talkative, I looked around to see what was going on. There was everything on the table—Scotch, bourbon, wines, and beer. We were having a wonderful time until Gowdy stood up across the table and looked at Butch and I. He saw we were just drinking beer, and he called us a couple of sissies.

I said, "What are *you* drinking?"

Gowdy said, "Devore and I are drinking Scotch and champagne chasers."

I said, "I never drink anything but beer." Gowdy said champagne was the best drink of them all. I looked at Butch and said, "Will we try some?" and Butch said, "Yes, if you will."

The first two glasses didn't taste so good. The next ones did, but I forgot to count. After starting on the wine, I remember shooting out imaginary lights on the way home. Butch lived at the same boarding house I did on Massachusetts Avenue, right near the ballpark. (We paid seven dollars a week for board and room.)

The next morning I awoke, and straight for the bathroom I went. My mouth was as dry as if I had just come across the Sahara Desert. I got started on that water and must have drunk a gallon when stars started to shoot out of my head and my head was going around like a dynamo. I met Butch at breakfast and he felt the same as I did. I said to him, "Do you think we can make it?"

He said, "We got to make it."

We arrived at the park, put on our uniforms, and went onto the playing field. I spotted that beautiful green grass with the sun beating down, and I said to myself and Butch, "Just the place for us to sweat this stuff out of us." We were basking in the sunshine when Butch nodded at me with a nudge and said, "Here's the Boss."

I said, "Turn over on your stomach and let me do the talking."

Stallings came by, stopped in front of us and bellowed at us, "What's the matter with you two?"

I said, "We ate some corn beef last night for dinner, and it made us both very sick."

Stallings said, "Go in and take a bath and go home and get a couple hours' sleep and I'm sure you will feel better."

The minute he was out of range we started for the clubhouse, only to run into Gowdy and Devore, the Scotch and champagne drinkers. They looked like they had come out of a bandbox, they looked so good. I said, "How do you do it?"

He said, "Lay off the drinking water and you will feel okay for this afternoon's game."

We went back to our boarding house, grabbed a couple hours' sleep, and laid off the water. I never was so thirsty in my life as the game we played that afternoon went ten innings. I was so thirsty that I was spitting cotton, or it felt that way to me. We got them out the first of the tenth and I was second man up in our half. I went right to the water fountain on the bench and the first man had already been retired and I was still drinking water. The boys yelled at me that I was up. I immediately yelled back at them, "Up where?" I was just like I felt the night before from drinking that water. Joe Connolly gave me his long bat and said, "Go up there and hit one, Rabbit."

I said, "Hit who? I'll fight anybody here." They finally got me started up to home plate and the first thing the umpire said to me was, "Rabbit, where have you been?"

I said, "None of your business; all you have to do is umpire."

He said, "Don't get too close to the plate, Rabbit; you are liable to get hurt."

I said, "Tell that pitcher out there to throw the ball."

"Strike one," said the umpire.

I said, "What do you mean strike; he never threw the ball."

"Yes, he did," said the umpire.

I said, "He won't throw any more by me." I saw the pitcher start to wind up and I started to swing at his motion when bat and ball met and it sailed over the left field fence. I stood at home plate when Gowdy rushed up to me and said, "Run, Rabbit; you made a home run and the game is over."

I said, "Run from who?" and he gave me a push and I stumbled around the bases touching them all.

In the clubhouse while I was undressing Stallings came over to me and said, "You go back to choking up; you are no home run hitter." Truthfully, I never did see the ball I hit, and years later Babe Adams, who was the pitcher that day, asked me if it was a curve or fastball I hit over the fence. I told him I never saw it and he said, "I know darn well you never did." [The game took place August 6. Rabbit did hit a home run to beat Adams in the tenth. However, he also got two singles and two stolen bases. The *Boston Globe* reported that he was sick.]

Getting Ahead in the Game

The other incident I spoke of happened when we were fast closing in on the Giants for first place. We were playing against Pittsburgh. Babe Adams was their pitcher. We went along for seven innings, nothing to nothing. I had been up to the plate three times and I couldn't see Adams that day as he was terribly fast. The result was I had struck out three times in succession.

I was going up to the plate on my fourth attempt to get on base when Stallings our manager yelled at me, "Come on, Rabbit, we got to win this ballgame."

I said, "I know it, but I just can't see this pitcher today."

Stallings said, "Remember McGraw's players, Herzog, Fletcher, and Snodgrass? They were all choke hitters like yourself. You know how they would stick out their arm, get their sleeve hit, and go to first base?"

(P.S. A choke hitter is a player who chokes his bat about half way up the handle and stands close to the plate so he can bend right over it.) [Maranville's note.]

I said, "Yes, I know that, but McGraw had long sleeves made especially for them so they could do that. I haven't got long sleeves, and furthermore I can't even see Adams' fastball."

Stallings said, "Okay, get on there somehow."

I saw Kid Elberfeld get hit on the side of the head many times, as he was a choke hitter, too. He would get a focus on the ball, and at the

On August 7, 1914, Boston Globe cartoonist Wallace Goldsmith
celebrated Rabbit's tenth-inning homer that defeated the Pirates, just
one of many hair-raising finishes for Stallings' men.

last second he would turn his head and the ball would ricochet off his head. I wasn't crazy enough to try that. As I neared the plate, I said to myself, "Well, I'll try sticking my arm out and getting hit as I can't hit this guy anyway." The first pitch I stuck my arm out, but I failed to get hit. The umpire to my surprise said, "Ball one." I said, "Well, I'll stick it out a little further this next pitch." Again to my surprise the umpire said, "Ball two."

I stuck my arm way out over the plate and the ball hit me right in the forehead between the eyes. I was knocked unconscious for about three or four minutes. I came to but was still groggy when Charlie Moran, who was the umpire, said, "Rabbit, if you can't make first base, they can put a runner in for you until you are okay again." I thanked him and started walking down the first base line, still groggy. I got about three-quarters of the way down when some big Irishman stood up and yelled at me, "That's putting the wood to it, Rabbit."

Falling for a Trick

Germany Schaefer was one of John McGraw's best lieutenants. [Schaefer, a longtime American Leaguer, was as famous as Maranville for his zany antics. Whether he was a friend of McGraw or not is not clear. Schaefer played 25 games with Washington in 1914 before joining the Federal League in 1915. Thus it is possible that he was in Philadelphia without a team in September 1914. In his manuscript, Rabbit's story moves back and forth between New York and Camden, New Jersey. Upon a close study of the record, it appears that the events described most likely took place in Philadelphia on the night of September 1–2 with the Braves a half-game behind the Giants. The details of the game were hazy in Rabbit's account, but the events of the night were vivid in his memory forty years later.] He had his girl as an accomplice. He introduced me to his lady friend. We went into the dining room and Germany had a good pull there with the head waiter and we were drinking real beer while the rest of the dining room thought we were drinking 1½ percent beer.

We stayed there until twelve o'clock when Germany's girlfriend asked me if I danced? I said, "Yes, I love to."

She then said, "Let's go over to Camden, New Jersey. They are open all night and we can eat, drink and be merry."

I said, "It's okay with me."

Germany said, "I'll have to renege as I have to meet a fellow in the morning on important business."

I said to Germany, "All right to take your girl over?" and he said, "Sure, Rabbit. Have a good time, both of you."

What Rabbit was to the National League, Germany Schaefer (left, with Merito Acosta) was to the American. When the two pranksters squared off, it was a battle of titans.

We arrived at some road house and were given a nice reception as everyone seemed to know her. Between eats, drinks, and dancing, I never noticed the time until the sun started to shine through the window. I looked at my watch and it said seven o'clock. I said to my girlfriend, "Let's get out of here; I have to play ball today."

I asked for the check, but she said, "Oh no, this party is on Germany and me."

When I walked into my room about ten o'clock, my roommate said, "Where the hell have you been until this hour?" I told him and he said, "You big sucker, that's one of McGraw's pet tricks and to think that you fell for that Germany Schaefer and girl act. Get to bed; you have been framed very nicely."

I awoke about one o'clock and went up to the park about half asleep. I never said a word about the frame on me.

After the game I called up Germany Schaefer. He still was in bed. I said, "Many thanks for your party last night. I had a wonderful time but today I paid for it."

Germany asked, "What happened, Rabbit?"

I said, "I couldn't hit a balloon if it was thrown up at me and I made three errors; I couldn't keep awake."

Germany said, "That's too bad. What was the score?"

I said, "Eight to three in favor of us, and I got three hits which drove in four runs and was all over that diamond. Next time you ever try to pull any more of your tricks on me, you better get a Dutchman like yourself, not an Irishman like me."

Charging into First

We were gradually gaining on the Giants, who were leading the league. We bought Herb Moran, an outfielder who was to add great strength to our ballclub. That was when the season was in its final half. It was then that Stallings started our double-shift outfield. From the start of that platoon system in the outfield, it paid off.

Mr. Gaffney [the Braves' owner] followed the club when we played in the east. We were playing a game in Brooklyn about a week before we were to take our last western trip when our manager

Stallings spotted Mr. Gaffney in a box seat. He walked over to him and said, "If you would go lose yourself and stop following this club around, we would win some ballgames."

Gaffney said, "Okay, I'll get out of here, and trust me, I will not follow you around anymore."

We finished our western trip and came back to Boston tied with the Giants. In those days, especially holidays, we played morning and afternoon. On Saturdays and holidays we played at Fenway Park, which was owned by the Red Sox, as our grounds [South End Grounds] were too small to take care of the crowds that we were drawing in. We beat Christy Mathewson, 5–4. That afternoon the fans broke down the fences and the mayor called the mounted police to drive the fans back off the field. Jeff Tesreau pitched for the Giants, and they beat us by a big score [10–1]. We had one more game with the Giants and we beat Rube Marquard 8–3. McGraw left the game in the seventh inning to make an early train back to New York, and as he was going into the dugout he yelled at the frenzied fans, "Nobody can beat that club now."

We won the pennant by 10½ ballgames, and were the most talked-of club in the sports world.

Psyching Connie Mack

The Philadelphia Athletics had won the pennant in the American League and they had what Connie Mack said was the best ballclub he had ever assembled. If you have forgotten, here they are: Stuffy McInnis 1B, Eddie Collins 2B, Jack Barry SS, and Home Run Baker 3B. Connie Mack called them the "$100,000" infield. Their outfield consisted of Rube Oldring LF, Amos Strunk CF, and Eddie Murphy RF. Their pitchers were Eddie Plank, Joe Bush, and Chief Bender; catchers, Jack Lapp and Wally Schang.

We arrived in Philadelphia two days before the World Series and we stayed at the Majestic Hotel on Broad Street. Some of the players walked over to the hotel as it was only a short walk from North Philadelphia, where we got off the train. On my way I saw an imitation ivory elephant [the Athletics were also called the White Elephants] in one of the curio shops and went in and asked the man the price of it. He said, "One dollar," and I purchased said elephant. I still have it with all the scores of the games we played in the Series marked on it.

The day following of our arrival in Philly, Stallings called a meeting of the club. We were discussing the weakness and the strength of the hitting power of the Athletics. We were down to the middle of their lineup when the bell in the telephone booth rang. I was nearest to it, so I answered. "Can I talk to Manager Stallings please?" I said, "Just a minute." I called out to Manager Stallings, "You're wanted on the phone."

He picked up the phone, and you never heard such a bawling out he gave to whoever he was talking to, who it later turned out to be Connie Mack, as that was what he told us when he came back to proceed with the meeting. He called Mr. Mack everything and said he was going to call the president of the league and tell him about his rules in baseball, that Connie Mack wouldn't let us have the park to practice on. (Note: there is a standing rule in baseball that the home team has to give the visiting team two hours the day before the Series opens to practice.) [Maranville's note.] It made us all very angry at Connie Mack, and we all said then and there, "Practice or no practice, we will beat them anyway."

Just before the meeting ended, the phone bell rang again and Manager Stallings answered it. "Manager Stallings, this is Mr. Mack and I am calling you to tell you that you can have the field from twelve to two PM."

Stallings roared back at him, "It's about time you got some sense in that pin head of yours," and hung up.

The next day we had our workout at Shibe Park, home of the Athletics. We always played in Baker Bowl, a little band box compared to Shibe Park. Shibe Park was a beautiful field. The infield was marvelous (not a pebble of any description on it). The outfield was like velvet. It was my first time in Shibe Park and I said to Johnny Evers, our captain and second baseman, "Anyone that misses a ball in this infield should be shot."

We dressed in the National League clubhouse and took taxis to and from Shibe Park. We had a wonderful workout and we looked like world champions, the way we snapped that ball around the infield and hit that ball to all corners of the lot.

Rabbit in the Lion's Den

After dinner I went up to my room and rested myself up as my ankles were in not too good of shape. About ten o'clock I decided a little air and a brisk walk would do me good. I started walking down Broad Street towards town. I was headed back to the hotel when I saw a big sign marked "Cafe" and, realizing I was thirsty, I pushed open the swinging door and went in. I should have been on a scouting trip. I never saw so many six-foot, six-inch fellows in my life. They were all longshoremen and ugly and tough as they make them. I was scared to death but like a real actor I went up to the bar and said to the giant bartender, "Glassa beer, please." I had my beer, turned, and looked the place over. They were all talking baseball. Some, for the Braves, the majority for the A's. I was having my second glass of beer when a fellow pushed up against me and asked, "Aren't you Rabbit Maranville?"

I said, "No." I said to myself, "I'm getting out of here. This party is going to get rough."

My friend said to the bartender, "Fill them up again." He did. I then bought one and after five or six more of the Dutch treat he asked me again, "You're the Rabbit for sure, aren't you?

I said, "Yes, I'm the Rabbit and who the hell are you?"

He said, "Just a minute," and he walked to the center of the bar. "Gentlemen, we have one of the Boston Braves in our midst, and it's no other than the Great Rabbit, their star shortstop." I took a bow from where I was standing at the bar and smiled.

About that time my friend introduced himself and he was Connie Mack's brother, proprietor of the place. He said, "Gentlemen, I'll show you what Bender is going to do to those Braves tomorrow." He imitated Bender's pitching form perfectly, only he was striking us all out.

I took as much of his pitching as I could when I walked over the center of the floor and said, "Get me a bat and I'll show you what we do to your ace Bender."

If they had let me go, I think I would be up there hitting yet as Bender never got anybody out. I then gave a little talk on what we were going to do to the Athletics in the coming Series. After a couple more of the "Delicious Grog" my friend Mr. Mack bet me and the whole crowd a steak dinner right after the Series.

I said, "That's a bet." I have never seen Mr. Mack's brother to this day.

I went back to the hotel, went up to my room and there was my roommate Johnny Evers with the pillows at the foot of the bed reading the papers.

When he saw me he said, "Where have you been to this hour?"

I said, "Just played the Series and we won at Gene Mack's Cafe downtown." I pulled the light switch out and away we went. I pulled it off; he pulled it back on. I don't know yet who got the last pull.

Boston Wins Game One

After our meeting for the first game of the World Series, the club decided that they wouldn't talk to the opposing players. We also said that we would ride them every chance we got. It started with Evers when they wanted to have his picture taken with Eddie Collins, captain and second baseman of the Athletics. Evers said to the photographer, "I wouldn't have my picture taken with that Pig Head if I never got my face in the papers," and he didn't.

Next it was Eddie Murphy, right fielder, saying, "Hello, Herbie" to Herbie Moran, our right fielder, as they were supposed to be good friends.

Moran said, "Don't hello me; I never talk to anyone that I haven't been introduced to."

Next was me, when Amos Strunk, the Athletics' center fielder, tried to go to second base after Schmidt, our first baseman, let a ball get about ten feet away from him. He picked the ball up, shot it to me, and I tagged Strunk sliding in. While tagging him I said, "Why don't you try running out of the ballpark?" What he called me I cannot put into writing. [Boston won the first game, 7–1.]

Boston Wins Game Two

The second game of the World Series was a thriller. Plank was the pitcher of the Athletics and Bill James was our pitcher. The game was 1–0 in our favor and the last of the ninth was the Athletics' last chance. They had men on first and second bases with one out with Eddie Murphy up. Murphy hadn't hit into a double play all year and was very fast. I was playing about ten feet from second base with Charlie Deal about twenty feet from third base. James was about to pitch when Evers called time. He looked at me and said, "Play closer to second base."

I moved over about five feet from second base. Deal moved over to me, putting third base wide open. I said, "Suppose he bunts or pushes a ball down the third base line? What then?"

Evers said, "He is a dead right field hitter and never hits to the left side of the diamond." James was just about to pitch when Evers again called time. He said, "Get nearer to second base."

I said, "You fathead, I'm almost on second base now."

He said, "Get closer."

I said, "Okay," and I moved over to within one yard of second base. Deal was practically playing shortstop. Evers then said, "Okay, James, go ahead."

The first ball James pitched Murphy hit like a rifle shot between James' legs. I put my foot on second base, reached out about a yard, and grabbed the ball with my glove hand and shot it to first base for a double play. If it hadn't been for Evers' insisting I play closer to second base, I would never have made the play, which seemed almost unbelievable to make from the spectators' point of view. Clark Griffith, President of the Washington club in the American League, said, "That's the greatest play I ever saw in my years of baseball." [The Braves won the game, 1–0.]

Boston Wins Game Three

The third game of the Series took place at Fenway Park, Boston, Massachusetts, and again it was a thriller. It was 2–2 going into the tenth inning. Wally Schang, the first man up, reached first base on a base hit. The next man up failed to sacrifice and struck out. [Next, both runners were safe on Eddie Murphy's grounder.] Oldring, on a hit and run play, hit a sizzling grounder to Evers, who knocked the ball down. The ball rolled about ten feet away. Evers retrieved the ball and came back into the infield (in the meantime, Schang was on his way to third base and Murphy to second). I yelled at Evers, who kept patting the ball in his glove. I yelled, "Third, Johnny, third!"

When Evers looked up and saw Schang, he was five feet from the base, so Evers could do nothing but tap the ball in his glove [and toss Oldring out at first. Baker singled in both runners off Evers' shin.] That made the score 4–2 in favor of the Athletics.

Coming off the field after the Athletics were out, Evers began crying like a baby. He reached the bench still crying when Oscar Dugey said to him, "What's the matter, Johnny?" Evers remarked about the big boner he had made. Dugey said, "Forget it, John; think of the games you won for us all season."

Hank Gowdy was our first man up in the tenth. He hit the first pitch of Joe Bush (who was pitching for the Athletics) into the center field bleachers for a home run. Herb Moran, next man up, drew a base on balls. Evers was the next man up. Some fans booed him while other fans yelled encouraging words to him. Here was his chance to make a comeback after the pulling of his boner. Evers hit one by the first baseman Stuffy McInnis and Moran went to third base. Joe Connolly, our left fielder, hit a long fly which scored Moran with the tying run. That was the end of our scoring in the ninth. We then went on until the twelfth inning when we scored one run to win the game. [Boston also won game four, 3–1.]

Rabbit's Stage Career

After the Series was over, I was offered a seventeen-week contract on the Keith Circuit. I did a coaching stunt that I did in the World Series and sang a couple of songs, finishing up with "Take Me Out to the Ball Game." I sang an Irish comedy song ("The Ha-Ha Song"). I forgot the words halfway through the song and I had to fake forgetting the rest of the week as it turned out to be a big laugh.

The third week out I played in Lewiston, Maine (Bill Carrigan's hometown; he was the manager of the Red Sox at the time). I was doing my coaching stunt finishing up with a hook slide, but the boards on the stage were uneven and when I went into my hook slide I turned my ankle and landed headfirst into the big bass drum. I saw the manager of the theater after and told him I couldn't go on and do my act anymore. He said, "Just take a bow, you're no actor anyway; all they want is to see you."

I finished my last week in Springfield, Massachusetts, my hometown. I played football that morning and opened up in the afternoon. From yelling so hard in the morning I became hoarse and could just about talk, but the manager of the theater insisted I do my full act. I tried to sing, but I was terrible. That night a big box party came in and they were feeling no pain. They heard my first song and one man yelled to the orchestra leader, "Stop the show." I tried to console the fellow, but he said to me in a quivering voice, "Rabbit, we are friends, and we bought you a big bouquet, not for your being a good actor, but for being such a lousy singer."

Rabbit and the Federal League

The Federal League tried to become a third big league in 1914. In every way possible they were snatching up American League and National League players to join with them. They would offer the players a big bonus and put it in the bank for them. They'd also give them an ironclad contract for three years. The American and National leagues made a rule that anyone jumping to the Federal League would be barred out of both leagues.

Bill Fleming, who was scouting for the Chicago club under Joe Tinker, made an appointment with Evers and me after the Series, and we met him. He laid down $100,000 in front of Evers and $50,000 in front of me as a bonus with a three-year contract to play for the Chicago Feds. Evers refused and so did I. Fleming wanted to know why we wouldn't jump as most every other player was. Evers said, "First thing is I am already signed up with Boston, and secondly when I sign a contract I live up to it. I have no respect for anyone that doesn't. Furthermore I am working for a man who owns our club (Jim Gaffney) and he is honest and square and has always been on the level with me and I shall do the same to him."

I spoke up and said, "Those are my sentiments too." People ask me today if I had it to do over would I have passed up all that money? I tell them yes, I would, as my word and signature on a signed document are of greater value to me than money.

Evers Apologizes to an Ump

It was at the close of the [1915] season when Johnny Evers our second baseman had a terrible argument with Bob Emslie (the umpire) over a play that wasn't even close and Emslie was correct on his call. Evers called Emslie everything under the sun and was put out of the ballgame. Evers and I came near blows after the game because I told him Emslie was right and that he was wrong and the language and names he called Emslie were disgraceful and he should apologize to him for the insults. That winter I received two letters from Evers telling me how he wrote Emslie a letter of apology and sent his children two big strapping dolls about four feet tall for Christmas.

The first day of the season the next year, Emslie was one of the umpires. Evers apologized to him and Emslie accepted it, but said to John with a smile on his face, "My daughters want to thank you for the beautiful dolls you sent to them last Christmas."

Johnny said, "That's fine. I am glad I could do something for you."

[Emslie replied] "Funny part of it all, Johnny, is one is thirty-five

"The Human Crab," Johnny Evers. Testy, high-strung, grouchy—all these tags fit him. So did team leader, money player, and best second baseman in the League.

and the other is thirty-eight years of age. They got a great kick out of your presents."

Double-Teaming Zimmerman

Playing in Chicago alongside of Johnny Evers, we had a real run in with Heinie Zimmerman, the Cubs' third baseman. It was along in the middle of the game with Zimmerman on first. He decided he would steal second base. Heinie had a very nasty slide. He would slide in with his left leg, then would twist his body and with a terrific kick with his right leg would kick you in the wrist. Many players had their wrist broken on his slides. Evers knew about this slide and would put his foot up in front of the bag, which would break Heinie's slide. This time, however, he forgot to block Heinie and took the throw from the catcher with one knee on the ground and, catching the ball with one hand, put the ball on Heinie's chin. It dazed Heinie for a minute, and when his view cleared away he grabbed Evers by the neck with both hands and started choking him.

I tried every angle to get at Heinie. I finally backed up about five feet and, with a running start and jumping into the air with my fist closed, landed on Heinie's jaw and down he went. Cy Rigler the umpire walked up to us and said, "You three are out of the game." Evers walked on one side of Heinie and I on the other. Heinie claimed that someone from our bench ran out and socked him and that he would get him later. Evers told him, "Rabbit hit you." But Heinie said, "No, he didn't; I know who hit me." We arrived at our respective clubhouses when Evers and Heinie started another verbal fight and were going to tear each other apart, but it never came off as we pulled Evers into the clubhouse.

The Merkle Play

Fred Merkle, the Giants' first baseman who is known to all baseball fans as Boner Fred, was in McGraw's opinion a smart, brainy ballplayer. His boner in failing to touch second base with two out lost the Giants a pennant in 1908. It could happen to any smart ballplayer. It happened this way: Johnny Evers was playing second base for the Chicago club. The Chicago club was playing against Pittsburgh in Pittsburgh. In the middle of the game Tommy Leach, the center fielder, was replaced by a rookie just breaking into the big league. The score was tied with men on first and third base and two men out. The batter singled, which drove in the winning run. After the game in the clubhouse, the rookie said to Johnny Evers, "Mr. Evers, that player on first base never touched second base."

Evers was furious and said to the rookie, "Why didn't you yell about it out there on the ballfield? It's too late now."

Evers on the next day asked Hank O'Day, who was umpiring back of the plate, if he saw that the player on first had failed to touch second base on that base hit that won the game. Hank truthfully answered that he didn't notice that he didn't touch second base as he said, "When I saw it was a base hit, I turned for the clubhouse figuring the game was over." [This account is at variance with accounts of the game published on September 4, 1908. In these, Evers did call for the ball, step on second, and claim a force-out. The umpire, however, had turned away from the field and failed to hear him.]

The Cubs then moved into New York to play their last series. Hank O'Day was again the umpire back of the plate. The same condition came up again with a man on third and Merkle on first base with two out. Al Bridwell, the Giants' shortstop, was up and he singled to center field.

Merkle, thinking the ballgame over, ran right past second base without touching it and ran to the clubhouse. Evers and O'Day were watching Merkle. Evers yelled to the center fielder for the ball and he threw it to Evers. Some of the Giants saw what happened on their way to the clubhouse [and] tried to keep Evers away from second base while others tried to steal the ball away from him. Hank O'Day stood still behind the plate watching everything that was going on. [He] finally saw Evers touch second base with the ball in his hand and waved Merkle out for not touching second base. The game ended in a tie and was played off in a game which the Cubs won for the pennant.

I have often thought if Hank O'Day had not been told about the play that happened in Pittsburgh he would not have seen Merkle not touching second base in New York.

P.S. If you will notice in the ballgames you go to, the player on base always runs to the next base, regardless of the score.

Outsprinting an Angry Crowd

Playing a game in St. Louis while I was with the Braves, the pitchers were knocking the players down as quick as they came up. We were leading by one run in the last of the ninth with two outs, and Bob Bescher, the center fielder for the Cardinals, was up. He was a big fellow 6'2" tall, weighed about 200, and was very fast. Pitcher Dick Rudolph took a couple of shots at Bescher, and out to the box he came and told Rudolph off. Rudolph said, "Get back there at the plate and hit."

Bescher said, "Yes, I will, but if you ever throw at me again I'll tear you apart."

With the count of 3-and-2 on Bescher, Rudolph walked in to Bescher at the plate and said, "Get ready to duck on this next pitch." The next pitch Rudolph made was a perfect strike and Bescher was out and the game was over.

Bescher was so mad that he was outguessed by Rudolph that he ran right to the box after Rudolph, who was no match for him. He was about five feet from Rudolph with fire in his eyes when I ran in and made a flying tackle that grounded Bescher, and Joe Connolly, our left fielder, and Butch Schmidt, our first baseman, sat on him. I grabbed Rudolph and we ran like hell to the clubhouse. The crowd chased onto the field and took after us. They didn't catch us, but they tried to get at us until about twelve o'clock that night, when the police came and broke it up and they took us back to the hotel in the patrol wagon.

An Aspirin Attack

I was playing a doubleheader in St. Louis one day while with the Boston club. The temperature was about 112 degrees after a tough night with some of the fellows on the club. I was leadoff man, and on the first ball pitched I hit a triple. I was weak when I got there, and what tasted so sweet the night before began to turn in my stomach. I scored on the next batter's base hit. I came in to the bench, a very sick man.

Stallings, our manager, looked at me and said, "Here, take these two aspirins. They will settle your stomach right away." I knew what I wanted and it wasn't aspirin. It was getting the sour beer out of my stomach. I took the two aspirin tablets but didn't put them into my mouth. I went to the back of the bench, put my finger down my throat and cleaned my stomach out good and I felt like a new man. I came from behind the bench to where all the players were sitting and I said to Stallings, "Those aspirin tablets always make me sick." I just wish you could have been there and seen all the players' hidden chuckles.

As I was having dinner with Hank Gowdy that night, he laughingly said, "So aspirin makes you sick, Rabbit."

I said, "Shut up, you prima donna; mind your own business."

Rabbit Goes to War

The 1918 baseball season was cut short owing to the war. I said to my pal, "Let's join the Navy." That afternoon we went over to the Charlestown Navy Yard and took our place in line with the rest of the recruits.

We were in line about one-half hour and had advanced about ten feet. I said to my buddy, "Let's get out of here and come back tomorrow." I was just about to get out of line when along came a big redheaded friend of mine. He spotted me and asked me if I was going to join up. I said, "Yes, I am," and before I had a chance to change my mind he said, "Follow me," and zip I was in the Navy.

The following morning we reported to the Navy Yard, received our sea bag and clothes and were assigned to our stations. I was assigned to a seagoing tugboat. We had a wonderful captain on our tug. He would let me off every day at noon and I would sell Liberty Bonds at the ballparks in the afternoon. I sold $250,000 worth of bonds that summer of 1918.

With all the professional ballplayers we had at the Yard, Captain Keis decided he would have a ballclub under Chief Jack Barry, who used to play shortstop for the Philadelphia Athletics. Captain Keis and Chief Barry held a meeting and figured they could make a lot of money for the Recreation Department, so they soon rounded up a good ballclub. They came to me and asked me to play on the team. I told them I didn't come into this outfit to play ball but to fight. After hearing of what my penalty would be for not obeying an officer, I decided I would play ball.

On that club were such players as Ernie Shore, pitcher for the Red Sox; Herb Pennock, pitcher, Boston Red Sox; Del Gainer, first baseman, Red Sox; Harold Janvrin, second baseman, Red Sox; Maranville, shortstop, Boston Braves; Mike McNally, Red Sox third baseman; outfielders: Whitey Witt, center field, Philadelphia Athletics; Leo Callahan, right field, Brooklyn; Chick Shorten, left field, Red Sox; Arthur Rico, catcher, Boston Braves; Jack Barry, manager. We played our first game on a Sunday at Braves Field to a capacity crowd of 56,000 people against Fort Devens of the Army.

Every ship that came into Charlestown Navy Yard we would have Chaplain Finn ask the captain if he would put in for our ballclub as we all wanted to go to sea. It wasn't long before Captain Keis had so many requests for us that he said, "Okay, I'll shanghai all of them, but they will not go together."

I was sent to the Atlantic Fleet along with Del Gainer and Whitey Witt. I went to the U.S.S. *Pennsylvania*, flagship of the fleet. Whitey Witt went to the battleship *Arkansas* and Gainer to the battleship *Minnesota*. Herb Pennock was sent to England along with Mike McNally, and Leo Callahan to France.

The U.S.S. *Pennsylvania* was like a big hotel. Took you a month to find your way about. I was assigned to Turret Three for my battle station. In a turret you have to start from the bottom and work yourself up. You go from powder room to pocket powder man, then to gunner, then to captain of the gunners. I was gunner of the left four-teen-inch gun when I noticed on one of our drills our pocket powder man. One time he would lift a powder bag (they weighed a hundred pounds apiece) almost over our heads; then the next one he would just about get up to us. I noticed this for a couple of days and, getting out of the turret after battle station drills were over, I said to our chief of the turret, "I'll bet you that pocket powderman of ours is using dope," and I explained what he had been doing.

The chief said to me, "That's a serious charge you are making without proof."

I said, "Okay, but I'll bet you he is a dopehead and I wish you would put someone to watch him."

He said, "I will, but let's keep this to ourselves."

In about two weeks they had the proof on him that he was a dopehead. He was having the dope sent to him in the form of powders. He was tried and found guilty and was given a dishonorable discharge from the Navy.

Rabbit Predicts a Celebration

We were in Norfolk, Virginia, on the tenth of November taking on ship's supplies making ready for going overseas. The following day, I was telling the boys of my division that they would get the big news tomorrow. Everyone kept asking me what the big news was going to be. I said, "Wait until tomorrow; I will tell you then." At six-thirty the next morning we got word that the armistice had been signed.

That afternoon of the signing of the armistice I was called in to the captain's quarters. The captain said to me, "How is it you knew the armistice was going to be signed today? Who gave you that information?"

I said, "I didn't know anything about the armistice being signed. The reason I said the big day is tomorrow and they would hear great news is that today is my birthday." With that the skipper laughed so much he almost fell out of his chair. When I reached deck the boys already had heard of my birthday, and did they give it to me! That was one birthday I will never forget.

A Room with a View

When Jim Thorpe came to Boston from the New York Giants in 1919 he picked me out as his roommate. I got a great kick out of it because I often wondered how an Indian scalped a white man. We were playing in Philadelphia. I was up in my room in my pajamas when my roommate Jim came in feeling no pain whatsoever. We were on the fourteenth floor. Jim started telling me of the wonderful time he had that evening and he got louder and louder. I said, "Shut up and turn the lights out and get into bed."

He said, "No, I want a drink."

I said, "There's no drink here. Go to sleep."

Jim said, "Give me a drink or I'll throw you out of the window."

Our second baseman [Buck Herzog] came into the room at that time when he heard Jim threaten me. Jim said, "You going to give me a drink?"

I said, "No, there's none here."

With that Jim grabbed me and putting me out the window said, I'll

Buck Herzog

It was said of Jim Thorpe that he failed in the big leagues because he couldn't hit the curveball. In his one year as Rabbit's teammate, he batted .327, so he must have been hitting something.

drop you to the pavement below if you don't give me a drink." There was a woman across from us just going to her room and saw Thorpe hanging me out the window. Herzog in the meantime grabbed the chamber pot under the bed and tried to hit Thorpe on the head but he missed Jim and the chamber pot landed on the pavement below making a terrible noise.

Thorpe said again to me, "If you don't give me a drink I'll drop you."

I said, "You big Indian, you haven't got the guts to." With that he pulled me back into the room satisfied I didn't have a drink for him.

In the meantime the woman who saw Thorpe putting me out the window called the office and said, "A man is throwing another man out of the window on the fourteenth floor."

We had just about got Thorpe shut up and the lights out when a terrific knocking came at our door and a big burly voice yelled, "Open the door; this is the police."

I yelled. "All right, I'll open the door, but what's the matter with you folks waking us up at this time of the night?" The cop told me what the woman had reported. I turned the lights on and said, "There's my roommate." (He was fast asleep.) "There hasn't been no noise on this floor that I know of." With that the cop left.

Checking out of the hotel looking at my pigeonhole [at the front desk], I saw a bill in there. I said to myself, "I don't owe anything; I didn't have no extras." With that I took the bill and read, "One chamber pot fifty cents." I paid it and never said a word.

Dodging Bullets in Hot Springs

In the fall of 1920 I was traded to Pittsburgh in exchange for Billy Southworth, Dinty Barbare, Fred Nicholson, and cash. They made the Pittsburgh ballpark over new and added new boxes. In 1921 I reported to Pittsburgh and took over that great shortstop Honus Wagner's job as he had retired from active playing, though he later became coach. [Howdy Caton, Zeb Terry, and others had played shortstop for Pittsburgh between 1917 and 1920 with little success.]

We trained in Hot Springs, Arkansas. We played a series against the Red Sox. The Boston and Pittsburgh scribes made a big hullabaloo about who was the best shortstop, myself or Everett Scott, who was Boston's shortstop. Some said I was and others believed Scott was. When the series was over there was a unanimous vote of the scribes that I was. Even Hugh Duffy of the Red Sox came to me and said, "Congratulations, Rabbit, I never saw such playing of shortstop in all my career."

In our exhibition games in the South, Dallas and Fort Worth, Texas, were among the cities we were to play in. We played Fort Worth first and moved over to Dallas after the game as it was only fourteen miles away. During our batting practice before the Fort Worth game our quartet sang three or four songs for the fans as they had heard us before. Our quartet consisted of Charlie Grimm, our first baseman, bass; Cotton Tierney, our second baseman, lead; George Whitted, our right fielder, baritone; Maranville, shortstop, tenor. To start a song we would have to wait three to five minutes for Tierney to get the slugs out of his throat before we could get the right pitch. We were so good that afternoon that the Elks who were having a sports night and dinner invited us to be their guests. We accepted, and for our dinner we again put the quartet to work to earn our grub.

Whitted ran into an old friend, Jess Hassell, who was president and half owner of the Dallas club. He said he would drive us back to Dallas as he lived there. We arrived at the Cleveland Hotel (where we were stopping) at three minutes of twelve. George Gibson, our manager, was waiting in the lobby for the night owls. Hassell came up to our room to use the telephone to call his wife to tell her he would be right home. Tierney and I had put on our pajamas and were ready for bed when our door was thrown open and a wild-eyed dame kept screaming, "Save me. Save me. He is going to kill me."

I pointed to a window and said, "Go through that window, and down the fire escape. You're not framing me."

About the time she was getting out of the window to go down the fire escape, a big bass voice outside the door bellowed, "Unlock that door and let me in or I'll shoot it open." All he had to do was turn the knob and walk in, but I guess he was so excited he forgot.

Hassell darted under the bed and Tierney got up on a radiator while I ducked into the bathroom and, sticking my head out a little, yelled to the guy outside, "What are you going to do?"

In 1921 the Rabbit was traded to Pittsburgh, where he had some fine years. He led the NL in double plays in 1923 and 1924—as a shortstop in '23 and, when Glenn Wright came in to play short the following year, as a second sacker.

He yelled back, "Shoot this door down."

I said, "Shoot your head off." He shot a .45-caliber right through the lock and it locked us in.

When Grimm heard the shot, he fell right out of bed and said, "That's Rabbit's room. Someone must have got shot."

The hotel was in an uproar. Everyone was telling us to open our door, which we couldn't do as we were locked in good. In about an hour they got a carpenter and he took off the whole lock and put a new one on.

In the meantime they had arrested the man. We later found out he was an oilman and had taken this girl out on a party and that she had stolen $800 off of him. The maid, the next day, found the $800 between the mattresses of their room. The party got his $800 back, but the complaints against him cost him much more than the $800.

The Pirates are Scuttled

It was in August that we came into New York with a seven-game lead over the Giants. Everyone was making a great fuss over us and congratulations came from all sides. I took it with a grain of salt, and it wasn't until George Gibson, our manager, ordered us down to right field to have our picture taken in a group that I exploded. I said to him, "Pictures for what? Wait until we win the pennant before we have our pictures taken."

The Giants beat us five straight, reducing our lead to two full games. We went from New York to Pittsburgh. I will never forget that booing we received from the fans as they quit on us cold. We had been going like a house on fire all year, and our slump came just at that time. No matter how hard we tried we just couldn't win. We went from first place in August to a tie with St. Louis in fourth place at the close of the season.

Rabbit Redux

Playing in New York [about 1922], we were rained out one day. Players of all clubs played cards, and it was a standing invitation for the home clubs to be the visitors' guests. We were staying at the Ansonia Hotel and every suite put up seven players. Philadelphia was playing Brooklyn and we were playing the Giants. That rainy afternoon the Ansonia Hotel looked like Monte Carlo with all the players playing one game or other.

I don't know how we got together, but Jack Scott, Hugh McQuillan, and Johnny Rawlings of the Giants and Dick Rudolph, Tony Boeckel, and I got to telling stories. Between stories we had a few pick-me-ups, and the different escapades we told were getting better and better. I used to wrestle quite a bit up home to keep in shape in the wintertime, and this friend of mine, Jim Barnes the middleweight champ, would teach me all the holds. I never liked Jack Scott, pitcher of the Giants, so I said to him, "I'll bet you that you can't put me on my back."

He being a 6' 3" fellow said, "Go away from me before I break you in two."

I said, "You can't do it."

The boys finally kidded Scott into wrestling me. Scott had the strength, but he knew nothing about wrestling. He tried everything he knew, but I outtricked him every move he made. I finally said, "I'll be down on my stomach; then see if you can put me on my back."

I took my position and he grabbed ahold of me. He put onto me a half nelson, then a full nelson and with his strength he had my chin touching my chest. As he added pressure I would change colors. It got so I couldn't breathe. I just couldn't do a thing as he had cut my windpipe off, and he would have strangled me to death if Tony Boeckel, who had seen me turning all kinds of color, hadn't grabbed Scott from behind and made Scott loosen his hold on me. It took me about three minutes before I could get my breath as I was gasping and choking. Johnny Rawlings was standing close by me when I said to him while choking, "Get me a little piece of soap." He slipped it to me unseen, and I started chewing away like you would chew a piece of

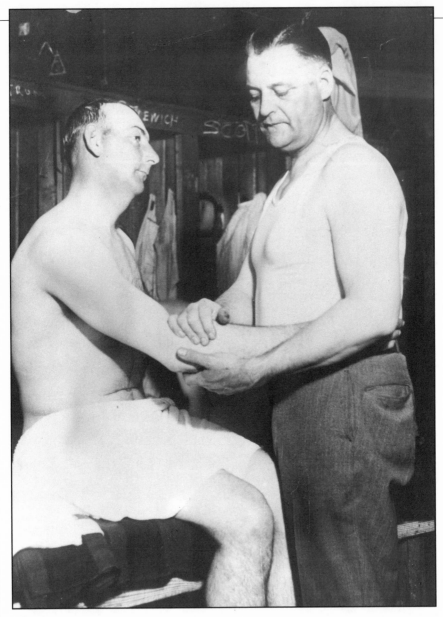

Doesn't pitcher Jack Scott, here getting a rub from trainer Doc Knowles of the Giants, look like a guy you could sell a bridge to?

gum. Soon I had a nice suds in my mouth and, giving Rawlings and Boeckel the wink, I started spitting the foam out; then, making out as it was my last breath, I fell to the floor in silence.

Rawlings was quick to get my act and he said to Scott, "You have choked Rabbit to death."

Hugh McQuillan came over then and said, "Let's carry him into his bedroom." Rawlings and McQuillan carried me into my room; they put me in my bed and covered me over with a sheet. All the players were in on the act by now but Scott, who was scared to pieces. Dick Rudolph said to the boys when they put the sheet over my head, "Let's kneel down and say a prayer for him as he was a great little guy."

They all got on their knees and Scott was with them praying out loud. "God, don't let Rabbit die; I didn't mean him no harm."

Rawlings then said, "Well, let's call the office and tell them what has happened. We have done everything we can up here."

Scott ran out of my room and up to his. Opening the door he screamed at his roommate, Art Nehf, the Giants' pitcher, "Give me a razor. I'm going to cut my throat. I've just killed Rabbit."

Nehf called our room and told us of what Scott was going to do and wanted to know if it was a joke or not. We told him it was a fact, Rabbit was strangled by Scott. Scott was like a lunatic looking all over the room for a razor. Nehf, in no friendly mood, called our room again, and this time we told him the truth that it was a joke. Nehf told Scott that it was a joke, and Scott, bursting into our room and seeing everyone laughing and me sitting up in the bed, he grabbed me and gave me a loving and hugging I never had before, saying, "Gee, I'm glad you're alive."

The next day while playing the Giants I tried to bend my neck over to pick up a ground ball, but it just wouldn't give. It took me over two weeks to get my neck loosened up from that full nelson Scott put on me.

The Red, White, and Blue

While we were playing in Philadelphia, Charles Pfirman, the umpire, and Manager Art Fletcher got into a real fight. Pfirman hit Fletcher over the head with his mask, which brought the fight to an end. When the fight started, Bob Hart, the first base umpire, ran to Pfirman's aid. He was right in the middle of the fight and got a real pushing around.

After the fight was over I went over to Bob Hart and said, "Bob, your face is all scratched up. Wait a minute and I'll get some Mercurochrome for you." (Bob didn't have a scratch on him.) I yelled into the bench and said, "Hey, bring out that Mercurochrome." I painted Bob's face until he looked like a zebra. The next day when Hart came on the field he came right over to me, and what he called me I dare not print.

Rabbit Foils the Cops

In the fall of 1924 I was traded along with Charlie Grimm (1B) and Wilbur Cooper (P) to Chicago for Vic Aldridge (P), George Grantham (2B), and Al Niehaus. In the fall of 1925 President Bill Veeck, Sr., asked me if I would manage the club for the last two months of the season, as Bill Killefer was called home.

I accepted the job, and at our first meeting I told the boys on the club what I wanted them to do. I said, "Boys, it's too late in the season to make rules, but one thing I insist on is to hustle on the ball field and win." We arrived in Brooklyn and my first game as manager we defeated Brooklyn.

The next day we were all at the park in uniform when the rain came and they called the game off. It was Prohibition in those days, and I didn't worry about my players drinking too much. I went back to the hotel. I dolled up a bit and decided to go see a friend of mine on Tenth Avenue who owned a speakeasy. He had a big police dog and had him trained to let you in, but you couldn't go out without the boss's consent to go out. I met my friend the proprietor and we had a beer together.

I was there a few minutes when a good friend of mine came in who was a detective. We had a few beers together when he asked me to make his rounds with him. I said, "No, I think I'll go back to the hotel." We had another beer, and looking through the mirror to my left were three of my ballplayers—Mandy Brooks (CF), Jim Brett (P), and Pinky Pittenger (3B). I said to them, "Drink up." I introduced them to my detective friend and asked them where they were going. They said, "Back to the hotel."

I said, "Okay, I'll ride back with you." We said good-bye to our detective friend and grabbed a cab. One of the boys (Jim Brett) said to me, "Do you mind if we stop at the Times Hotel?"

I said, "No," so we put out for the Times Hotel. (During our ride the boys would take my name Rabbit in their conversation quite often.) We pulled up at the Times Hotel and Brett and Pittenger asked the driver what the fare was. He asked an enormous fee, and the boys said they wouldn't pay it. Brooks and I were in the back seat when we saw Brett take a punch at the cab driver. He made a punch at Brett while Pittenger tried to kick him in the stomach. The cab driver yelled, "I'll get you, Rabbit," and I jumped out of the cab and went after him. He was an old retired fighter, I found out later. We were at it tooth and nail, and where the people came from I don't know. Then the cops came and all I saw was cops using their nightsticks on our heads. The cops got Pittenger and Brett, but Brooks and I got lost in the crowd.

I was standing in front of the old Wallack Hotel on Broadway when a captain of police walked up to me and asked me if I was Rabbit Maranville. I said, "Yes, I am."

He said, "Do you mind riding with us to the station to recognize a couple of fellows who they say are your ballplayers?"

I said, "Sure," like a dummy I was. I no more got in that wagon when I knew I was in for it along with the other two. Brooks in the meantime had been hit over the head by one of the cops and knocked unconscious. Some good Samaritan grabbed him and pulled him over to his car and put him in it. Brooks regained his senses in Central Park, where the friend was giving him plenty of air to recuperate him. The cab driver was thrown in with us and we were locked up. They put the three of us in one room and the cab driver next to us. You can imagine what we called each other from room to room.

I said to the cab driver, "If I get you outside alone, I'll kill you." I tried to get the use of the telephone for four hours and finally after spending $40 I got ahold of my detective friend.

We arrived at night court, and on my way I sat right opposite this big fat sergeant. I said to him, "Well, you big fathead, you put your foot into it this time."

He said, "What do you mean?"

I said, "I'm going to sue the city." (The law says policemen shall never use their nightsticks unless for a riot call.)

We were put in a big room. I was smoking a cigarette when some hophead came up to me and said, "Hi, buddy. Give me a cigarette." Before I knew it he had the cigarette from my mouth and I wanted out of that place right away.

My fat Irish sergeant came in and said to me, "If you don't press that riot charge to the judge, we won't press any charges against you."

I said, "It's okay with me but no double-crossing," which he lived up to.

We were the judge's first case for the evening. Brett was the first one to the stand.

"What's your name?"

"Jim Brett," said Jim.

"Haven't I seen you before?"

"Maybe," said Jim, "but not in here. I'm a ballplayer."

"Sure," said the judge. "I've seen you pitch plenty of times at the Polo Grounds. You play there tomorrow, don't you?"

And Jim said, "Yes, your Honor, we do."

He then said, "Well, get out of here and get a good night's sleep so you can play tomorrow."

Pittenger was next and practically the same conversation took place with him being sent back to his hotel. I was called upon next. Judge said, "Name," and I told him. "What are you doing here?"

I said, "I don't know."

The judge said, "You can't make vestpocket catches in here, and I want to see you make some tomorrow at the Polo Grounds."

I was discharged like the others when our mutual friend the cab driver took the stand. The judge gave him a good tongue-lashing when the cab driver shouted, "Rabbit says he is going to kill me when he gets me outside alone."

The judge said, "Rabbit is not going to kill you because you are fined $5 and one night in jail." I knew I couldn't have been mistaken as I said to the judge, "Aren't you Judge McQuade, McGraw's partner?"

And winking his eye at me, he said, "That's me, Rabbit. I will be up to see you at the Polo Grounds tomorrow."

Alexander Lets the Rabbit Down

With me as manager of the Cubs, we had won two straight. It was at the Polo Grounds after our first victory that I figured on pitching Grover Alexander. He was taken sick, and McGraw called an ambulance and we took him to the hotel. The papers of New York ate me up for not pitching Alexander, as it was the first time he had ever came to New York without pitching one or two games against the Giants. We kept his sickness a secret, which made the newspapermen furious.

On our way to Philadelphia, I didn't have one pitcher available, and we had a five-game series in three days. I scratched my brain trying to figure out who I could start. I finally said, "Boys, listen, who will volunteer to pitch today in Philly?"

Alexander spoke up and said, "I'll pitch, Rabbit."

I said, "How can you pitch? You just got out of bed and you're weaker than a cat." He said he was okay.

I said, "All right, you pitch the first game and you can have off until Saturday and you can pitch the first game of that doubleheader."

He pitched and won. Saturday came and I was on the field warming up when Bill Veeck, president of the club, called me over to his box and I saw Mr. Wrigley, owner of the club, sitting alongside of him. He asked me who was pitching and I told him Alexander. He said, "Where is he? He isn't on the field." I went down to the clubhouse, but there was no Alexander. After the games were over without signs of Alexander, as he never showed up at the ballpark that day at all, we went back to our hotel and packed, as we were leaving for Chicago that night.

I was up in my room packing when our secretary, John Seys, came in and said, "Mr. Veeck left this for you before he left for Chicago."

He handed me a piece of paper and it read, "Fined Alexander $250 and you and he report to my office on your arrival in Chicago."

I said to Mr. Seys, "Where the devil is Alex? I haven't heard a word from him and can't imagine where he is."

Mr. Seys said, "I think I know where we can find him."

We got the telephone of the party where we found out that he was and I asked for Alexander. He came on the phone and I said, "Alex,

Grover Cleveland was the toughest pitcher Rabbit had to face until finally, in 1927–28, they became teammates on the St. Louis Cardinals.

this is Rabbit. Get up to that station and get into your berth and don't speak to anyone."

I arrived up at the train early and immediately went to Alexander's berth and he was in bed. He was anything but in shape, and I said to him, "Well, you got yourself and me in a fine mess pulling what you have done." I said to him, "The more I try and be a good fellow with you, the more you abuse a fellow."

We arrived in Chicago and went straight to Mr. Veeck's office, I said on the way up to Mr. Veeck's office, "Tell him the truth about what you did."

Mr. Veeck gave him a tongue-lashing and in return Alex told him a pack of lies. Mr. Veeck said, "That settles it. You have not only cost the Rabbit his job but you're fined $250 more for your falsehoods."

George Gibson took the club over the next day, and everyone wanted to know why I got fired. I never said a word to anyone about what happened in Mr. Veeck's office and never did while I was playing. Alexander tried later to pull the same stuff on Joe McCarthy [manager of the Cubs 1926–1930] when he said, "I'm bigger than you, McCarthy, around here" and McCarthy said, "Okay we will see." The following week Alexander was sent to St. Louis.

Rabbit Plays Russian Roulette

In the fall of 1925 the Chicago Cubs asked waivers on me. Brooklyn claimed me and I reported to Clearwater, Florida, to Manager Wilbert Robinson. My roommate was Jack Fournier, our first baseman. (He was the first of any first basemen who wore sun glasses).

Zack Wheat, the left fielder, became sick, and I went down to cheer him up. It was prohibition days at the time. Zack asked me if I knew where he could get a quart of whiskey as he wanted to use it in a medicinal way. I said I didn't, but we were going over to the Belaire Hotel, and I would see what I could do for him. Bernie Neis of the Braves, Mickey O'Neil, and myself went over to the hotel, and we sat in the cocktail lounge. We were waiting for a waiter when a man came over to me and said, "Hello, Rabbit."

I said, "Hello, how are you?"

He said, "I guess you don't remember me." I said I didn't. He said, "I used to know you in New York at the Commodore Hotel, where you fellows used to stay."

I said, "What are you doing here?" He said he was the steward and he had sent about ten cases of Scotch up to Judge Landis' room. I said (in a pitiful weak voice), "Can a fellow get a drink around here?"

He said, "Sure, anything you want." We had a few drinks when I asked him if I could get a couple of quarts as I promised Zack Wheat I would bring him one if I could get ahold of one. He said, "Have as many as you want." I paid him for the precious liquid and we went back to our hotel in Clearwater. We arrived there and I asked the boys up to have a cocktail. I left them in my room and took the bottle down to Wheat's room as I promised. I went back to my room and there was a crowd in there. O'Neil, Neis, Eddie Brown, Dave Bancroft, and some rookie I didn't know. Neis was feeling pretty high when he started to go through Fournier's trunk, which was not locked.

I said to Neis, "Don't go in that trunk. That's Fournier's and he will raise the devil if he finds out someone has been in it and blame me."

Neis laughed at me and opened the top drawer. Out he came with a pistol. He said, "Rabbit, I'm going to shoot you."

With the pistol pointing at me I said, "I'm a Navy man, I'm not afraid to die." With that he pulled the trigger.

There was a click when Brown grabbed the pistol and said to Neis, "Never point a gun at anyone." With that he pointed the pistol to the floor and pulled the trigger. You could hear the shot all over the hotel. He then examined the pistol and found the five chambers loaded except the first one that Neis had pointed at me.

After that shot was fired, you couldn't count up to ten before the room was cleared empty. Brown, Bancroft, and the rookie headed it back to St. Petersburg where they were training, while Neis, O'Neil, and I took to the streets in different directions.

I told Fournier about the incident that night, and he said, "I always keep my first chamber empty as a fellow is liable to be too fast on the draw sometimes." I thanked the Lord that the first chamber was empty or I would probably have had a gob's burial in Clearwater Harbor.

Uncle Wilbert Robinson

Robinson, our manager at Brooklyn, was a grand old man and more of a father than of a manager. His favorite pets were Dazzy Vance, Jesse Petty, and Fournier. We were having a meeting before the game in the clubhouse and he said, "Petty, you are the pitcher today."

Petty spoke up and said, "Robby, I didn't get in until three o'clock and I feel tired."

Rabbit never played for "the Little Napoleon," John McGraw (left), and it would have been interesting to see how he took to McGraw's discipline. The easy-going, lovable Wilbert Robinson had his fill in less than a year.

Robby said, "Okay you can pitch tomorrow."

In the extreme corner of the Brooklyn bench was a big square box with a telephone resting on it for communications from the office to Robby. When the game started, Petty went right down and sat next to the box and put his left arm on the box, which was a perfect resting place for a lefthander, which Petty was. It was but a few minutes when he was fast asleep, known by every player but not Robby. Boston had us beat about four to nothing in the fourth inning when we were putting on a rally. We had three men in and three men on base, and we were yelling and pounding the bats up and down on the bench when Robby happened to look where Petty was and saw that he was sound asleep. At once he yelled to us, "Stop all this yelling and pounding of those bats. If you wake that guy up, he will give us more hell than all our competitors put together."

Who's on Third?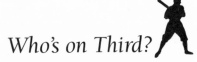

Boston came to town the next day and unbeknown to me was to see the funniest play I ever saw in baseball. It happened this way. With one man on, Dazzy Vance got a base hit to center field. The next man up tried to bunt but popped up and was out. Chick Fewster was the next batter up and was hit by a pitch. Babe Herman was our next batter. He hit a terrific line drive to right field. It looked like the fielder would catch it, but it went over his head against the right field wall. Herman, when he hit the ball, started running with his head down and his chin on his chest. Fewster was standing off about ten feet from first base, waiting to see if the ball was going to be caught. When he saw the ball go over the fielder's head he started for third base. When he got to where the shortstop plays, Herman passed him and went right on to third base with a beautiful hook slide. Fewster kept on running and went into third base with a hook slide on the opposite side of the base from Herman. Vance, who was halfway home, turned and saw Herman and Fewster on each corner of the base and ran back to third with a dashing belly slide that put three men on third base at the same time.

Robby said to me on the bench, "What's going on down there at third base?"

I said, "There's three men on third, and if they stay there long enough I'll go down and join them and make a quartet out of it."

A Near Triple Killing

It was in Brooklyn that I had my chance to make a triple play unassisted. We were playing against St. Louis. They had three men on base and no one out. Ray Blades, the Cardinals' center fielder, was the batter. With the count three and two on him and everyone running, he hit a terrific line drive about two yards away from me. I got a good jump on the ball and, stretching wide with my glove hand, caught the ball and touched second base for two out, and ten feet away from me was the runner that was on first.

Chick Fewster, who was our second baseman, said, "Touch him, Rabbit."

I looked at Chick, tossed him the ball, and said, "You tag him; you may as well get in on this triple play with me." Chick tagged him and the reporters wrote me up furiously for not making the triple play myself. I was always a team player, not an individual. My motto was to win as a team player always.

Rabbit Runs for the Jewels

I was with the Brooklyn club, and we were going on our last western trip of the season. Mrs. Rabbit traveled with me and I told her to be all ready after the game as we were making an early train. She packed her duds and even put in the family jewels. We arrived at Penn Station and, getting off the subway, I said to her, "Didn't you have more bags than that?"

She said, "My God, I left it in the subway car, and all my jewels and our securities are in that bag."

The subway train was beginning to move and pick up speed. I ran alongside the train and came across an open window and dove in. The people in the car were startled. I made my way down to the seat I figured we had and a big fat woman was occupying the space. I pulled up her dresses and, putting my arm underneath between her limbs, I grabbed the bag. I was just about to straighten up when I received a crack on my chin which knocked me right on the floor. I knew then that trying to explain to her was all out, so I walked to the other end of the car with a tight grip on my bag.

The next stop was Seventy-second Street, and I ran up the subway stairs, grabbed a cab, and said, "Penn Station as fast as you can make it." I was just on the runway to the train when I saw my wife and Manager Robinson stepping onto the train and it began to move. I yelled, "Keep the door open." I ran as fast as I ever did in my life, probably faster, and I made the train. Mrs. Rabbit, with all the excitement and seeing me with the bag with all her possessions, fainted in Manager Robinson's arms.

Rabbit Is Rich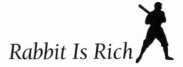

In 1926 on our last trip to Chicago, Whitey Witt, our center fielder, and I were told by Robinson that he had to release us as we were getting too much money. I said, "I am tickled to death. I never was on such a screwy ballclub in my life." We shook hands and parted.

That fall I was offered a lot of jobs as manager of minor league teams but I turned them all down.

Along about January 1927, I received a letter from my old manager, George Stallings, who was now manager of the Rochester club in the International League. He offered me a good salary and $2,500 for signing, payable on the Opening Day of the 1927 season.

The Opening Day of the season came, and I went up to the club's offices and saw Manager Stallings. I said to him, "Well, today's Opening Day. How about my $2,500 as per our agreement?" Manager Stallings told me that they didn't have the money and asked me if I would go along with him until such time as they had it and he would pay me. I went along with him for two months when I went up again to the club offices and demanded my money or I would quit the club and sue them for my money. I listened to Manager Stallings' tale of woe, and soft-hearted Rabbit again went along with him, believing in his word to come through with my money.

It was about three weeks later that I heard of Scout Barrett of the Cardinals club being in town looking for a shortstop. St. Louis was only a few games behind first place. It didn't interest me as I never trusted Branch Rickey [Cardinal general manager], although I always thought him the smartest man in baseball. Barrett was around asking questions about me. Was I in good shape, was I drinking, staying out late at night, etc. Herb Moran, our right fielder, told him I was in great shape, having a great year, and hadn't had a drink in over a year. Barrett came to me and said, "Rickey wants you for his ballclub right away."

I said, "Tell Rickey to go jump in the lake; I'm not interested."

About three days later I came home from the movies. There in the front room of my home were Rickey, Stallings, and Hicks, owner of our club. I asked the Mrs. what they were doing there. She said, "They want you to go to St. Louis."

I said, "Nothing doing."

Rickey said, "Get packed, Rabbit; we can talk contract on our way to the train as it leaves soon."

Hicks then spoke up and said, "Yes, Rabbit, it's a great opportunity for you."

I turned on him like a cat on a mouse. I said, "Pay me that $2,500 you owe me or everything is out."

Rickey spoke up and said, "I'll pay it, Rabbit, if he don't."

I said, "Oh, no, you don't pull that Stallings stuff on me anymore. I'm not leaving this house until I am satisfied." Mrs. Maranville begged me to get packed and I said to her, "Do you want me to go to St. Louis?" and she said, "Yes, I do."

I didn't get the $2,500, but she did. So as long as it was in the family I should worry. I talked contract on the way to the station, also about a bonus for signing, which was agreeable to both parties. If Rickey had come to Rochester two weeks sooner, everyone said St. Louis would have won the pennant. Pittsburgh beat us for the pennant by 1½ games.

The Pennant-Winning Cards

That year of 1928 was one of the closest races in baseball. We would be in first place one day by a half-game, the next day in second place by a half-game, and it went that way right down to the finish.

My roommate was that Wild Horse of the Osage, Pepper Martin. He would carry in his wardrobe one shirt and one pair of socks. No pajamas. Pants and shoes made up the rest. Every night he would wash his shirt and socks. Never had his shirt ironed the whole eastern trip. Going to bed, he would undress to the nude and in two minutes be fast asleep. On a scenic railway [roller coaster], he would stand up and give one of those Oklahoma cowboy yells going down those steep drops. He had more nerve than anyone I ever knew. We were in first place by a half-game when he said to me, "I'm going down tomorrow morning and buy me a camping outfit, automobile, and trailer, and pay for it on the World Series money."

I said, "Suppose we don't win? How you going to pay for all that stuff?"

He said, "I don't know." He went downtown the next day, bought himself an auto, trailer, rods, guns, ammunition, and a sleeping outfit. He said, "Whole business cost me $4,800."

We were going into the seventh inning with the score tied when I looked at the scoreboard and saw that Chicago was trimming the Giants. I said, "If we win this game, we go into first place by a full game." I yelled at the players, "Come on, let's have some pep. Let's go." It had its effect, and before we knew it, we had three men on base and no one out. Syl Johnson, our pitcher, was our next batter. I was talking to Clarence Mitchell, one of our pitchers, when I saw Johnson step into the batter's box. I said to Mitchell, "What the hell, he isn't going to let Johnson hit?"

Mitchell said to me, "Looks like it. What are you going to do about it?"

I said, "I'll show you. This means $5,000 to me and I can use it. I ran out to where [manager Bill] McKechnie was coaching at third base. I said, "Bill you're not going to let this fellow hit, are you?"

McKechnie said, "He hits one now and then."

I said, "Now and then! Put a man up there who can hit. This means the pennant for us and about $5,000 apiece."

During our argument Frankie Frisch and Jack Onslow, our coach, came up to us. They asked what the argument was, and McKechnie told them. They agreed with me and McKechnie said, "Well, who have I got to hit?"

I said, "Ray Blades."

The umpire came down then and said, "Break this up and play ball."

After more arguing McKechnie finally put up Ray Blades for Johnson. Blades walked; that forced in a run. When the smoke had cleared, we had scored seven runs. New York lost to Chicago, and we went into first place and never lost it.

A Promise from Rickey

We were to play the New York Yankees in the World Series. The day before the Series, Rickey, vice president of the club, called me up to his office and congratulated me on my playing of shortstop and winning the pennant for them on our last eastern trip. He also asked me what I would consider for relinquishing my right to an unconditional release? I told him I didn't know, I hadn't given it a thought. He said, "Think it over and come up to my office tomorrow morning and let me know."

I went up to his office the following day. Rickey said, "Did you think it over?"

I said, "Yes, I did."

Rickey said, "What did you consider your unconditional release worth?"

I said, "$7,500."

He said, "Fair enough. I have a contract all ready for you to sign, for when you get through being active we plan to have you manage one of our farm clubs."

I looked the release over and said, "Where is Mr. Breadon's signature?" (He was president of the club.) Just then Mr. Breadon was going from one room to another when Mr. Rickey asked him if he

Branch Rickey with a product of his farm system. Actually, this chicken probably liked Rickey better than Rabbit did.

would sign the release. Breadon said, "I'm very busy and my word is good enough, isn't it?"

I said, "No, it isn't, not for me. I want it down in black and white. I'm sick of being the fall guy."

Rickey then said, "You're on this ballclub to stay, and furthermore we will get this unconditional release fixed up."

The Promise Broken

We opened the World Series in New York, and the Yankees beat us the first two games. We then moved on to St. Louis, where they beat us the next two games. I believe I am the only player that has ever been on a club that won four straight and lost four straight in a World Series. I also hit the same in each Series fourteen years apart—.308.

I got $2,907 for my share in the 1914 World Series against the Athletics when we won four straight. In 1928, when the Yanks beat us four straight, I received $4,680 for my share. Sometimes it's better to lose than win.

After the Series I went out and bought Mrs. Rabbit a Studebaker car. We were home in Rochester no more than two days when Mrs. Moran, the wife of our right fielder in the 1914 World Series, called the Mrs. and said to her, "See where Rabbit was waived back to Boston."

That winter I received a letter from Rickey saying there was a lot of things in baseball that he had no control over and that the two mistakes he made in his life were when he let Hornsby and myself go.

The next year I was with the Boston club when we played an exhibition game against the Cardinals at Avon Park, Florida, Coming onto the field, we had to pass the Cardinals' box, where Mr. Breadon and Mr. Rickey were sitting. As I was going by the box, Mr. Breadon said, "Hello, Rabbit."

I looked at them both with their sarcastic smiles on their faces and said to them, "I don't talk to damn liars."

Stallings' Last Word

It's a funny thing that your favorite saying will be with you to your grave. George Stallings was death on a pitcher who would give bases on balls. Another one of his rules was get that two-and-two ball over the plate.

In 1929 Stallings was taken very sick up at Montreal, Canada. No one doctor could diagnose his case. He was getting worse every day. Mrs. Stallings decided to take him back to Haddock, Georgia, his home, where if he did die it might comfort him in his last days on earth. They had Mr. Stallings in the ambulance and were on their way to Haddock when the doctor said to Mrs. Stallings, "What caused this trouble in the first place?" Mr. Stallings was in a coma during this conversation.

Mrs. Stallings said to the doctor, "I don't know. I have had all the specialists in Canada, and not one of them could tell the cause of his trouble."

Mr. Stallings came out of his coma for about ten seconds, looked up at the doctor and said, "Bases on balls, you fathead, was the cause of it all." He passed right back into a coma, and two minutes later the doctor pronounced him dead.

Boston Braves manager George Stallings, "the Miracle Man," sits alongside Johnny Evers. He behaved with the decorum of a Southern gentleman off the field, but in the dugout he was a foul-mouthed bully.

Rabbit Runs into a Jam

In 1929 under the management of Judge Emil Fuchs, we were having a real hectic game in Philadelphia. Everyone was pulling one bad play after another. It was in the eighth inning of the ballgame with the score tied, two men on, and one out. I was the next batter up. I got a base hit to left field scoring George Harper, which turned out to be the winning run. As I turned first base and stopped about ten feet from it, I looked into left field and saw Lefty O'Doul making bluff throws to third base. I said to myself, "Throw it, throw it, and I'll go on to second base."

He finally threw the ball to third base, and I scampered to second base with a beautiful hook slide. I was just coming up to my feet when I saw Joe Dugan, our utility man, looking down at me and he said, "What the hell you doing here?"

I said, "I don't know, but I'm going right back to first base." On the way back to first base they caught me. I'll dare not tell you what adjectives were shouted at me, and they also threw in some fancy nouns.

How to Hit Carl Mays

Playing at the Polo Grounds, we were to face Carl Mays, who came to the Giants from the Reds. There was a sellout at the Polo Grounds and the day was ideal for baseball. Barry McCormick was the umpire back of the plate. It was the first time I had ever faced Mays, as he was tough for a righthanded hitter to hit. He threw what they called a submarine sidearm ball which was hard to follow.

The first ball Mays threw to me was across my shoe tops, and the umpire called it a strike. I didn't say anything but gave him a dirty look. The next ball Mays pitched was about the same place as the first pitch, and again Umpire McCormick called it a strike.

I said, "Get the ball up; I'm not that small."

He said, "Get in there and hit."

I said, "Get the ball up." I then got down on my knees and with my bat on my shoulder I yelled to Mays to pitch. He was laughing so much at me that he couldn't pitch.

McCormick came walking out in front of the plate and said, "Get up there and hit."

I said, "You're not going to call any more low strikes on me."

McCormick said, "Get up on your feet or I'll put you out of the game."

I said, "Oh no you won't." He said he would. I said, "What constitutes a strike?" (From the knees up to the shoulders.)

Mays still couldn't pitch because of his laughing, so after a couple of minutes I stood up and took my natural stance. The next ball Mays pitched I singled to left field for a base hit. I started to run down the first base line, pulled out my handkerchief, and while waving my handkerchief to the stands I skipped the rest of the way to first base. I never looked back at McCormick because if I did I was a dead duck to be out of the ballgame.

Helping a Friend

In 1928, when I was on a road trip with St. Louis, we had with us a sporting editor by the name of Jim Gould. He was about 6'3" in height, weighed about 240 pounds and wore one of those big Texan hats. He was a dyed-in-the wool booster for the Cardinals. That night at the hotel he decided to have a party all by himself. I think he visited the room of every player that was on the club. He dropped into my room and when leaving forgot his Texan hat. I asked him if he had written his story, and he said, "No." I told a friend of mine to send it in and sign my name.

When we got back to St. Louis, the editor said to Gould, "You are relieved of your present job and back to a plain reporter."

It was in 1930 when I ran into Jim Gould again. He said, "Rabbit, you have got to give me a story, not a plain one but one that will have to do with the future." I told Jim I had given him every story I knew, but he said, "Oh, think of one for me because I can get my sporting editor's job back if I come up with a live story."

I said, "All right, come over to the hotel this afternoon, and I'll try and think one up."

Jim came up to our room and asked if I had thought of a good story. I said, "No, I can't think of any."

My roommate said, "Why don't you tell him about your 1914 drive?"

I said, "I have told that a million times already."

Jim said, "That won't do; we published that before."

I was undressing to take an afternoon nap when I suddenly compared the St. Louis club to our 1914 club, that is, if they had the hustle. I spoke up quickly, "Jim, I got you a story."

He said, "What is it, Rabbit?"

I said, "Your St. Louis club is just 7½ ballgames out of first place, and they have to swing through the East again, then come back to St. Louis and finish out the season." The St. Louis club had Gabby Street as their manager.

Gould said, "What of it if they have to go east and finish at home?"

I said, "Do you mean to tell me that ballplayers like Frisch, Bottomley, Wilson, and Hafey are hustling? Not in my book they're not. If that club would go out and hustle from now on to the end of the season, they would win the pennant easily."

Jim wrote the story up, didn't pull no punches. All these fellows I named were good friends of mine, but when I got onto the field, not one of them would talk to me. I finally got to Jim Bottomley, and he said that the fellows were as sore as the devil because I gave out that story to Jim Gould.

I said to Jim Bottomley, "Get those fellows over here and I'll tell them off." Jim got them together after a little coaxing, and I said to them, "Everything I said to Jim Gould stands, and if you fellows want to throw $6,000 away, that's your business. But I'll bet any one of you anything you want that if you do get out there and hustle like you should you will win the pennant easy." When I left them I was still their friend and they were mine.

They won the pennant and Jim Gould for his story was given his sporting editor's job back.

Rabbit Prevents a Riot

Playing with the Boston club in Chicago one day we had a real exciting game. The two clubs were not too friendly toward each other, and when the Cubs' pitcher threw a ball at our catcher [Al Spohrer], that set off the fireworks. He said to the pitcher, "If you ever throw another ball at my head, I'll hit you over the head with this bat."

The Cubs' pitcher stood on the rubber and laughed at him. That was enough. Out from the batter's box he marched toward the pitcher's box. Players rushed to the pitcher's mound from both clubs. I was right back of the pitcher, and if he started to hit [Spohrer] I was going to give it to him good. I was waiting when Wes Schulmerich, our right fielder, came up behind me, grabbed me by the collar, and said, "Get out of here, little boy; I'll take care of this fellow." Schulmerich was 6' 2", 190 pounds.

I decided then that seeing as I couldn't get back into the middle of things, I would go over to the first base coaching box and put on a fight of my own. I went over there and started shadow-boxing with myself. I got so excited in my workout that I gave myself an uppercut and knocked myself out. The fans in the meantime had turned from the argument in the pitcher's box.

About eight o'clock the next morning my phone rang in my room. Leslie O'Connor was on the other end of the wire. (He was Judge Landis' secretary.) He said, "Good morning, Rabbit; Judge Landis wants you down to his office right away." While dressing I said to my roommate, "What's that old goat want of me so early in the morning."

I arrived at the judge's office in about fifteen minutes, and Leslie O'Connor rushed me into his chambers. "Good morning, Rabbit. I didn't call you down here to congratulate you on the show you put on at first base, but to say that you stopped a panic by your quick thinking to draw attention to you instead of to the start of a free-for-all fight at the pitcher's mound. Again I congratulate you for saving the day, which would have turned out to be a serious situation. That's all."

I looked at him and said, "You called me down here at this hour in the morning to tell me this?"

He said, "Yes."

I said, "Give me my taxi money and I'm going back to the hotel and get some sleep. This is the middle of the night for me."

Another Old Trick

Playing in Cincinnati as a member of the Braves, I ran into a very sad and embarrassing situation. It was the first of the ninth inning, with Cincinnati ahead by one run. I was the first hitter up and I got a base hit. I was sacrificed to second base and was the tying run. Pfirman, the umpire, was in an argument with Harvey Hendrick, the Reds' first baseman. Pfirman yelled at me, "Tell him what I did to Manager Fletcher in Philadelphia, Rabbit."

Tony Cuccinello was playing about two yards off second base when I noticed him. I said, "What are you trying to do, pick me off?"

Tony said, "No." I took another step away from second when, *bing*, I saw the ball go over my shoulder to Tony, and I was picked off second base on that old hidden-ball trick.

It's a long walk from second base to the bench, and the riding the fans gave me I can hear yet. We had twenty-five men on our ballclub. Twenty-three of them were on the bench. When I reached the bench, I asked, "Who threw the ball to Tony?" Not one of the twenty-three men could tell me. We lost the ballgame by one run.

On our way to the clubhouse I passed Manager McKechnie, who had been coaching at third base. He said to me, "If you would keep your eyes open, we would win a game sometime."

I was furious. I said, "All right, you were coaching at third base. Just who did throw that ball to Tony?"

He said, "Durocher."

I said, "You're as blind as the rest of your ballclub; Durocher could never have thrown that ball from the angle at which it was thrown." We had quite an argument, and it lasted even under the shower bath when I said, "I'm going over to their clubhouse and find out just who did throw the ball." I put my shorts on and over to the Cincinnati clubhouse I went. Dan Howley, manager of the Reds, said, "Looking for the ball, Rabbit?"

I said, "Don't try to be funny." I went right over to Joe Stripp, the

Reds' third baseman, who was unwrapping about ten yards of adhesive tape from his legs which kept them together. I said, "Joe, did you throw that ball to Tony?" and he said, "Yes, I did, Rabbit." I said, "I knew you did; it couldn't have come from any other angle."

McKechnie and I went back to our hotel together. I was still mad at being caught off second base. I just couldn't shake it off. I had my dinner alone that night. I had finished my dinner, all but my dessert, when the head waiter came over to me and, putting down a delicious melon à la mode, said, "Compliments of Manager Howley."

I said, not very friendly, "Tell him many thanks." I started eating the ice cream and melon and had just about enough of it when I struck something hard in the ice cream. I thought it might have been a piece of ice, so I dug deeper into the ice cream and getting under what I thought was a piece of ice was a little ball about the size of a golf ball, and written on it was, "Here is the hidden ball, Rabbit." If I could have got ahold of that Manager Howley, I would have given him an awful beating. As I got up to leave the dining room, everyone in the room was giving me the great big laugh.

A Fishy Story

On our last western trip in 1915 our club was in Chicago. Coming in from the ballpark after the game, Butch Schmidt, our first baseman, asked me, "Where are you going to have dinner?"

I said, "I don't know—anywhere that the food is good." Butch said, "Let's eat at the Boston Oyster House," which was only a couple of blocks away from our hotel in the Loop.

We went in and the hostess came up to us and said, "This way, boys."

We were seated at a table for two when the waiter came up and said, "Are you ready to order?"

I said, "Bring us two seidels of beer." We finished the two seidels and Butch ordered two more. The waiter came with the two seidels and we gave our order. The second seidel started to crawl up on me and made me feel pretty good. I looked around the dining room, and right next to me was this little fountain with three goldfish swimming around in a circle. The waiter brought in my clams and I ordered two more seidels of beer. We finished the two and I had my clams about gone when I said to Butch, "I'll bet I can harpoon one of those goldfish with this clam fork."

Butch said, "You couldn't even hit the fish, not saying anything about harpooning it."

I said, "Okay, take a look." I took a good aim at the back of the goldfish's mouth and let the fork go. It struck perfect right behind his mouth. He swam around the fountain with the fork in the back of his neck. Just about that time the hostess looked over at us.

Butch said, "She's coming over here." When the fish came around again, I grabbed the fork, and fork and fish came right out of the fountain. Butch said, "Get rid of that goldfish or she will raise the devil."

I took the fork out of the goldfish and put him on my plate. I grabbed a knife, cut his head and tail off and shoved them in my pocket and ate the rest of it. By that time the hostess had arrived at the table, took a look at us, then looked at the fountain with the goldfish. "Gentlemen," she said, "'There was three fish in that bowl; now there is only two. What did you do with that other fish?"

We said, "We don't know anything about your old fishes, so why pick on us?" One word led on to another and the result was that we made as if we were highly insulted and we left the restaurant.

Schmidt, on his way back to the hotel, kept saying, "You couldn't do that again if you tried for fifty years." I told him I thought he was right.

At age forty-four, Rabbit managed Elmira of the New York-Penn League, played everyday shortstop, and hit .323.

Who Was Rabbit Maranville?

by Bob Carroll

Rabbit Maranville died on January 5, 1954, only a few weeks before he was elected to the Baseball Hall of Fame. He would have been pleased, though not surprised, by his election.

Although he was perhaps the poorest hitter ever enshrined there for his on-field exploits, Rabbit's wizardry with a glove made him a highly valuable major leaguer for twenty-three seasons and at times *the* most valuable.

George Stallings thought so. The Rabbit's manager when the "Miracle Braves" won the 1914 World Championship, Stallings called him "the greatest player to come into the game since Ty Cobb." That was hyperbole, of course, inspired by the Braves' "impossible" World Series win over Connie Mack's Philadelphia Athletics. Next to Cobb's .367 lifetime average, Rabbit's .258 just doesn't compare. But the 5'5" (some say 5' 4½") Maranville stood as tall as nearly anyone. At his death Rabbit held five major league records and four other National League marks, all but one related to fielding.

Yet had he been only an ordinary player, Maranville might still have earned a plaque at Cooperstown, a special niche reserved for famous "characters" whose zany exploits have made baseball more than a contest of bat, ball, and glove. Colonel Jacob Ruppert, the New York Yankees' owner, described Maranville as the funniest man he ever saw in baseball.

Rabbit was born in Springfield, Massachusetts, November 11, 1891, the third of five children. His mother was Irish, but his policeman father and the Maranville name were French. Fifteen-year-old "Stumpy," or "Bunty"—he had not yet received his enduring nickname—dropped out of high school after one year to be an apprentice tinsmith, but he preferred ballplaying to showing up for work.

He played for various semipro teams and in 1911 signed with New Bedford of the New England League for a princely $125 a month. Tommy Dowd, the New Bedford manager, had spent ten years in the majors playing second base and outfield for a variety of teams, including the infamous Cleveland Spiders of 1899, perhaps the worst team ever to disgrace the National League. He paid Maranville $750 for the season but charged him two months' pay for an insurance policy.

Rabbit hit a sickly .227 and committed 61 errors. But some of those old New England League infields had more rubble and holes than a construction site. And the gloves were useful only in shielding the hand; they didn't aid a fielder as today's traps do. Finally, scorers were less forgiving then. Any ball touched was either an out or an error, and Rabbit got to more balls than anyone except the chief packer at the Spalding plant.

Rabbit's reputation as a flake was probably born in New Bedford. The following story has been told many times and placed in just about every major league city, but it probably happened there. Or perhaps it only happened there first.

Supposedly, Rabbit and a couple of other players were walking to the ballpark on the far side of a river. "What are we walking up to the bridge for?" he asked. "We could save ten blocks by swimming across the river." He thereupon dived in, fully clothed.

(Many Maranville stories are hard to confirm, such as the tale that he once crawled out onto a hotel ledge to try to grab a pigeon.)

At the end of 1912 Rabbit joined the last-place Braves, along with another rookie, Miguel "Mike" Gonzalez, the Cuban catcher who later added the pithy scouting report "Good field, no hit" to baseball's literature. In 1912 Gonzalez caught only one game, and John McGraw's Giants stole four bases. Shrugged Mike: "She run. I throw. She safe."

One day in Brooklyn the rookie Rabbit took a pitch that he recognized as a ball despite umpire Bill Finneran's dogged insistence that it was a strike. Rabbit thereupon took a pair of glasses from his pocket, polished them carefully, and handed them to the ump.

George Stallings took over as manager in 1913. Stallings was a cultured Georgia plantation owner who could be urbane and charming in a drawing room, but on a dugout bench he became a madman. He could ride opponents unmercifully and just as easily use his sadistic tongue to rip his own players so profanely that he'd make even John McGraw blush. His most printable epithet was "bonehead." One day, needing a pinch hitter, he growled to his bench, "Now you, bonehead, get up there and bat." Seven Braves leaped to the bat rack.

On the bench Stallings was all fidget—tapping his foot, getting up, resitting, or sliding along the plank. He slid so much that he wore the seats out of four pairs of trousers in a normal season and five in 1914.

Although an educated man, Stallings was monumentally superstitious. If a Brave got a hit, he would freeze in that position until the next out. His greatest fear was paper lying on the field. Opponents, particularly Heinie Zimmerman, liked to torture him by walking past the bench tearing a sheet of paper into tiny pieces and strewing them behind him. It is said that once, while George was bending down to pick them up, he heard the crack of a basehit and froze. The batting rally lasted fifteen minutes, and Stallings was in bed for a day with a sore back.

Maranville quickly became one of his favorite players. Second baseman Bill Sweeney had a weak arm and couldn't make the throw home on a double-steal attempt. So Stallings, the master psychologist, insisted in Rabbit's hearing that only the second baseman could make the play successfully, while coach Fred Mitchell insisted that the shortstop should make it. As they argued, Rabbit broke in to say he could *so* make the play. The next night he threw two runners out at home. "I showed Stallings," he crowed triumphantly.

Stallings would receive his "Miracle Man" moniker for the glorious events of the following year, but he began earning it in 1913. Without a .300 hitter (John Titus led the team with .297), George brought the Braves in fifth. It was their best showing since a third-place finish in 1902 and the first time they'd finished out of last place since 1908.

Said Stallings: "Give me a ballclub of only mediocre ability, and if I can get the players in the right state of mind, they'll beat the world champions. But they've got to believe they can do it."

Most of the players on the 1914 team were brought in by Stallings. Tall Hank Gowdy, the hard-throwing catcher whose strongest comment was a heartfelt "Criminy sakes!" was rescued from the minors.

But his biggest coup was second baseman Johnny Evers, who had learned to win with the Cubs' champs of 1906–08 and '10. Johnny used the threat of jumping to the Federal League to muscle a $25,000 signing bonus out of the Braves, but in 1914 he was worth his weight—125 pounds—in gold.

Evers wasn't the hitter to rank with the American League's Nap Lajoie and Eddie Collins. But in the field he was the equal of anyone, and his most valuable asset was his fiery disposition. He and Stallings were a matched set, quiet and courteous off the field but holy terrors on it.

Maranville and Evers meshed into a brilliant double-play combination. Though no poet wrote immortal doggerel about Maranville-to-Evers-to-Schmidt, Johnny and Rabbit made more DPs than Joe Tinker and Evers ever had. Evers turned 73 of them in 1914, compared to only 29 with Tinker in 1909. Maranville was in on 92, compared to Tinker's high of 73.

Stallings' platooning of his outfielders is probably the earliest example of wholesale platooning, and one of the most effective.

Aside from the middle infield, the Braves' strength was in the three pitchers, who started 107 of their 158 games. Dick Rudolph, a 160-pound righthander, led the league in wins with a 27–10 mark. Another righty, Bill James, at 6'3" enjoyed his only outstanding season, but it was a beaut—26–7 and a 1.90 ERA. Lefty George Tyler, perhaps the Braves' best southpaw until Warren Spahn, went 16–14.

From July 7 on, when the Braves began their drive out of last place, the hard-luck Tyler was 7–7 with five shutouts, including a 0–0 tie; Rudolph was 13–1, and James 15–1, including two 1–0 shutouts. No one else won more than five games that year, although a rookie from Harvard, George Davis, hurled a no-hitter.

Joe Connolly at .306, was the only regular over .300. Rabbit's 78 RBIs led the team, and his 74 runs were second to Evers' 81. He led all shortstops in assists and set a modern (post-1900) record for putouts.

The Braves not only won the pennant by 10½ games, they whipped the vaunted A's, seeking their fourth straight world title, in four straight.

At season's end Evers won the Chalmers Award as the National League's MVP. Maranville finished second.

In Macon, Georgia, the following spring, Maranville and Sherry Magee disrupted a Holy Rollers' meeting, fled from the cops, and ducked into a Salvation Army Band, where they quickly borrowed a tambourine and a drum, while the nickels and pennies rained onto the drum.

In 1915 Evers tore up his ankle and played in only 83 games. James suffered a shoulder injury that all but ended his career. Once more on July 4 they found themselves in last place, and again they rallied.

The Rabbit kept the team loose.

One evening Rabbit borrowed a bellhop's uniform to deliver a fake telegram to Stallings and found the manager in his bath. Stallings barely glanced at the bellhop. "What are you waiting for?" he snapped.

"My dime, you cheapskate," Rabbit replied, as Stallings leaped from the tub and, clothed only in bubbles, chased him into the hall.

On a hot day in St. Louis—and it can get very hot there—Maranville suddenly yelled, "The heat! The heat!" and dived full-clothed into a pool in the hotel lobby. In some accounts, he came up with a goldfish in his mouth, hollering, "He bit me, so I bit him back!"

This time, however, the miracle fell short, and the Braves finished seven games behind the Phils and Grover Alexander.

In the spring of 1916 Maranville instigated a strike among the players. The Braves' exhibition schedule had the players sleeping on trains for twenty nights in a row. In protest, they stopped shaving and wore only blue working shirts with loud neckties and bizarre caps. When Rabbit and two others walked into a store in Georgia, the owner phoned the sheriff to report three jailbreakers. The Braves promptly changed their schedule to give the boys some nights off the train.

Jim Thorpe, the world's greatest athlete, once steamed into second base, where Rabbit tagged him out. "You little shrimp! You blocked me!" Thorpe, the ex-football player, cried, leaping up.

"Go back to the dugout, you big ape," Rabbit replied, "before I punch you in the mouth."

"Why, you sawed-off runt!" Jim bellowed. "I'll kill you for that."

"Yeah?" said Rabbit, "and you're just the guy who can do it."

Thorpe turned and trotted off the field, grinning.

Evers was injured again, and at thirty-four his career was as good as over. Yet by Labor Day the Braves had moved into first place by .002 in a three-way fight with the Dodgers and Phillies. Brooklyn finally took the pennant when Boston and Philadelphia killed each other off in a six-game series at Philadelphia.

The Rabbit's hitting was down to .235, but his 79 runs led the Braves. He also led the league in fielding percentage, putouts, and assists.

The Braves fell to sixth in 1917. The next year, with Maranville in the Navy for nearly all the season, they dropped another notch, to seventh. He returned in 1919 and pulled them back to sixth again.

On May 1, 1920, the Braves played one of the most famous games in history, a twenty-six-inning tie against Brooklyn, the longest game ever played in the major leagues. Rabbit was 3-for-10.

After a day off, they played nineteen more innings before beating the Dodgers, who nevertheless went on to win the pennant.

The Braves fell back to seventh with a .408 percentage, the lowest of Stallings' eight years as Boston skipper. George resigned in November, and in February Boston traded Rabbit to Pittsburgh.

Pirates owner Barney Dreyfuss brought the Rabbit to the Steel City in the spring of 1921 to meet the fans and press. Dreyfuss spoke in tones so low you'd have thought he was discussing ship convoys amid a nest of spies. "At first," Rabbit told the crowd, "I had some difficulty understanding what Mr. Dreyfuss was saying. But when he handed me my new contract and I saw the fine salary he had written into it, we understood each other perfectly."

Rabbit gave the Pirates their first reliable shortstop since the great Honus Wagner had retired. With the new lively ball, he also batted an unheard of (for him) .294, scored 90 runs, batted in 70, and ended with the highest fielding average he had yet attained.

Pittsburgh spent the summer in first place, as Rabbit clowned with Jolly Cholly Grimm, Cotton Tierney, and Possum Whitted.

Grimm told of one pitcher who refused to throw another pitch until he got a drink. While Cholly, Cotton, and Rabbit huddled around him (Possum was in the outfield), a flask magically appeared, all four of them took a pull or two on it, and the game resumed. "What was going on out there?" manager George Gibson asked in the dugout.

"Oh," said Rabbit, "his supporter was binding him and he didn't know what to do in front of all those people."

Noting the popular "flapper" look, the boys took batting practice with their socks rolled down, and no warm-up was complete without a song or two. They even had an offer to take their act on the vaudeville circuit, should Pittsburgh win the pennant. But, as New York manager McGraw observed, "You can't sing your way through this league."

In late August Pittsburgh took a seven and a half-game lead into the Polo Grounds for a five-game series against the Giants. New York won all five and went on to take the flag without warbling a note.

Dreyfuss blamed the collapse on the players' hijinks and hired Bill McKechnie as manager sixty-six games into the 1922 season. Barney warned him that he had "a couple of wild Indians" on the club—Chief Yellowhorse, a Pawnee Indian pitcher, "and that Irish Indian, Maranville." McKechnie promised to solve the problem by rooming with both of them. Returning to the room one evening, McKechnie was astonished to find them both in bed and snoring. He opened the closet door and was nearly knocked down by a flock of pigeons.

Rabbit opened one eye. "Heh, Bill, don't open that other closet," he said. "Those pigeons belong to the Chief. Mine are in that one over there."

Maranville had a great year, setting personal highs in fielding, batting (.295), and runs (115), as the Pirates finished in a third-place tie. They finished third again in 1923.

In 1924 Maranville faced the most formidable rival of his career, young Glenn Wright, who had a better arm and could hit rings around him. So McKechnie moved Rabbit to second base. With Grimm, Maranville, Wright, and Pie Traynor at third, the Pirates had a dream infield that would make Connie Mack's old $100,000 combination look overpriced.

Wright led the team in RBIs and the league in assists, while Maranville, at his new position, set a new record (since broken) for chances by a second baseman. In 1923 he had led the league in double plays by a shortstop; this year he led in DPs by a second baseman.

Unfortunately, the Pirates' pitching was weak, and when the Giants kayoed them three straight in the Polo Grounds in September, they were locked into another third-place finish.

In the MVP vote that year, Rabbit led all the Pirates, just ahead of Kiki Cuyler, who hit .354.

But Dreyfuss traded Maranville and Grimm to the Cubs, happy to be rid of "my banjo players."

In the spring of '25 a newspaper photographer found Maranville and Grimm on the golf course. He posed Grimm flat on his back with a tee in his mouth, while Rabbit stood over him ready to take a swing.

Click!

Whack!

Rabbit said later it was a beautiful drive over the photographer's head and down the course, but Grimm was definitely not jolly.

The Cubs were in seventh place under manager Reindeer Bill Killefer, when owner William Wrigley gave the manager's job to Rabbit. Maranville's managing (23–30) was not as disastrous as sometimes painted—the Cubs had played about the same under Killefer. They would probably have done better if Rabbit's star short-stop, Maranville, had not broken his leg halfway through the season.

Still, at thirty-three, Rabbit was too much one of the boys to crack a whip, and too much of a drinker to instill sobriety in such world-class boozers as Pete Alexander. Unfortunately, his brief and riotous term was no doubt embellished, as all Maranville stories are, and he was never again allowed to manage a major league team. It recalls another fella who was considered too much the clown to be anything but a failed manager until the Yankees hired him in 1949.

A famous story has Maranville scooping the Chicago press on his firing as manager by standing outside Wrigley Field and pretending to hawk newspapers while yelling, "Extra! Extra! Maranville Fired!"

(This may be only a variation on an earlier story when Bill Klem tossed him out of a game. In this version he was outside Ebbets Field in full uniform a few minutes after, yelling, "Extra! Read all about Maranville and that big baboon, Klem!")

In November the Rabbit was waived to Brooklyn for the 1926 season. He would seem to have been perfect for the "Daffy Dodgers" of those days. Under popular, easygoing Wilbert Robinson, Brooklyn achieved a reputation for wildly wonderful insanity. Alas for their fame, the Dodgers, were also popular with the opponents.

Pitcher Dazzy Vance formed a group christened the "4-for-0 Club," derived from a typical Vancian day at bat. The chief bylaw was "Raise all the hell you want but don't get caught." Rabbit became a member almost from the day he arrived. Dressed in sheets with towels wrapped turbanlike around their heads, they meted out justice to all members who were guilty of getting caught.

In 1927 Rabbit went to Rochester, where he announced that "The national consumption of alcoholic beverages took a sharp downturn after May 24, 1927. That's the day I quit drinking." He hit .298 there and won a trip back to the major leagues with the Cardinals.

Rabbit was convinced he'd "won" the 1928 pennant for the Cardinals. Others agreed that his presence was the most significant change between 1927 and 1928. He hit a mere .240 but formed a solid double-play duo with Frankie Frisch—perhaps they were the best combination in the league since Maranville and Evers thirteen years earlier. In the MVP vote he was the second-highest Redbird, second only to Jim Bottomley, who won the award. But when the Cards lost the World Series in four straight to the Yankees, both Maranville and manager McKechnie were fired.

Bill McKechnie was Rabbit's manager at Pittsburgh and St. Louis.

The Rabbit returned to Boston in 1929 and had his best season in years—.284, 87 runs, and a chances-per-game average over 6. Not bad for a guy considered washed up three years earlier! But a pitching staff with a horrendous 5.12 ERA practically guaranteed the team last place.

With McKechnie managing and Wally Berger hitting a rookie record 38 home runs (no other Brave hit more than 5), Boston rose to sixth in 1930. At thirty-eight, Rabbit hit .281 and led all shortstops in fielding again.

In '31 Berger hit half as many homers and the Braves fell back to seventh. But Rabbit played in 145 games, the oldest regular in the league.

After the season he joined an all-star team to Japan. The infield was Lou Gehrig, Frisch, Maranville, and Willie Kamm; Al Simmons and Lefty O'Doul were two of the outfielders; Mickey Cochrane caught and Lefty Grove and Larry French were pitchers. They sailed over on a Japanese liner with a Japanese naval delegation headed by an admiral who took a liking to Maranville, a former sailor himself. One day while the admiral napped in a deck chair, Rabbit painted a face on his bald head.

Rabbit was the Japanese fans' favorite player. He kidded them, and they kidded him back.

At one souvenir store, Gehrig spotted him admiring a large ivory elephant, but the $150 price was outside Rabbit's budget. At a big Armistice Day party—Rabbit's fortieth birthday—a huge gong was struck forty times, and servants placed a large package before him. Inside was a series of smaller packages. The last one contained the ivory elephant.

Back in Boston in 1932 the Braves were next-to-last in runs, but their no-name pitching staff was second in ERA, and the team led all league clubs in the fewest errors. Rabbit, again at second base, posted his highest fielding average ever. He didn't play it safe and wave at the tough ones; he led all NL second basemen in putouts.

The next year the Braves won 83 games, their most since 1916. Rabbit's batting average was down to .218, but again the Braves made fewer errors than any team in the league.

At the advanced age of forty-two, Rabbit was ready for another season in 1934, but he broke his leg sliding into home in spring training. On hearing the news, humorist Will Rogers called it

"America's greatest crisis." It was Rabbit's third broken leg, but this one didn't set right, and he was out for the season. Mail poured in, including some proposals of marriage. In September, 22,000 fans gave him a "day" at Braves Field.

He tried to come back but played only 23 games in 1935.

In '36 he took over as player-manager in Elmira, New York, of the New York-Pennsylvania League team and hit an uncharacteristic .323. In ensuing years he managed Montreal, Albany, and Springfield. He was later director of the New York *Journal-American*'s baseball school. One of his pupils, pitcher Billy Loes, went up to the Dodgers and turned out to be almost as flaky as Rabbit had been.

The Rabbit's Place in the Pantheon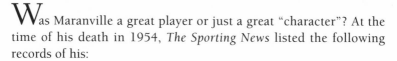

W̶as Maranville a great player or just a great "character"? At the time of his death in 1954, *The Sporting News* listed the following records of his:

Major league

Most chances accepted, shortstop	12,471
Most putouts, shortstop	5,133
Most assists, shortstop (modern)	7,338
Years leading league, putouts, shortstop	6
Longest errorless game, shortstop	26 innings
Most at bats, doubleheader (tie)	13

National League

Most games, shortstop	2,153
Most years 500 assists, shortstop	5
Most years played	23
Most chances, season, shortstop (modern)	574 (1914)
Most years leading league, assists (tie)	5

In *Total Baseball* Pete Palmer and John Thorn do not rank him among the top 500 players. That puts him below such luminaries as John Titus, Oyster Burns, and Fritz Ostermueller. This is shocking.

Even Rabbit's greatest supporters don't pretend he was an outstanding hitter. Timely, yes. Outstanding, never. Rabbit hit only 28 home runs in his career. But curiously, he slapped 177 triples, as many as Stan Musial and more than Rogers Hornsby, Joe Jackson, or Lou Gehrig.

Maranville's reputation was earned with his glove. Yet even in fielding, Palmer and Thorn rank Maranville no higher than sixty-third. *Total Baseball* may have most players pegged within a linear inch of their actual worth, but with Maranville it's wrong.

In his *Historical Baseball Abstract*, Bill James ranks the Rabbit tied for tenth among all shortstops in "career value." He writes:

> *There are some considerations that argue in Rabbit's behalf as a great player. One is the mere truth that he was able to play regularly in the major leagues at the age of forty-one while hitting .218, with no homers, for a contending team. This fact seems to be consistent only with the most formidable of defensive skills.*

Furthermore, James points out, Rabbit always did well in MVP voting. And when Rabbit was lost to the Braves' infield in 1934, the team ERA went up by more than a run!

Such men as George Stallings and Bill McKechnie never questioned his value. After all, a run is a run, whether it's driven in with a bat or prevented with a glove. A man who handles six balls a game in the field might account for as many wins as one who bats four times.

Another point to consider in arguing Maranville's greatness was his record in Hall of Fame balloting. He wasn't one of those Veteran's Committee pats on the back that have often been highly criticized. From 1937 until his election in 1954, the baseball writers—many of whom had seen him play—always gave him a significant number of votes. In the 1954 election, he garnered the top votes total, outpolling fellow electees Bill Dickey and Bill Terry.

In other words, it's not those who actually knew what Maranville could do on a diamond who question his right to a place among baseball's immortals. Only those who must rely on numbers printed on a page have doubts. Perhaps they should have a little faith in the perceptions of the Rabbit's contemporaries.

The Hall of Fame has been ponderously slow in recognizing

WALTER J. V. MARANVILLE
"RABBIT"
BOSTON, PITTSBURGH, CHICAGO,
BROOKLYN AND ST. LOUIS,
NATIONAL LEAGUE, 1912 – 1935

PLAYED MORE GAMES, 2153, AT SHORTSTOP
THAN ANY OTHER NATIONAL LEAGUE PLAYER.
AT BAT TOTAL, 10078, SURPASSED BY ONLY
ONE NATIONAL LEAGUER, HONUS WAGNER.
MADE 2605 HITS IN 23 SEASONS. MEMBER
OF 1914 BOSTON BRAVES "MIRACLE TEAM"
THAT WON PENNANT, THEN WORLD SERIES
FROM ATHLETICS IN 4 GAMES.

Rabbit was inducted into the Baseball Hall of Fame in 1954, too late for him to enjoy the honor.

players for their defensive contributions. There are enough big bats at Cooperstown to make up a league of designated hitters. You can even find a few enshrinees who were liabilities in the field. For the most part, the superior fielders—Wagner, Speaker, Mays and so forth—came in on their bats while lip service was paid to their gloves.

Maranville's plaque hanging in the hallowed hall of Cooperstown reads:

> Played more games, 2,153, at shortstop than any other National League player. At bat total, 10,078, surpassed by only one National Leaguer, Honus Wagner. Made 2,605 hits in 23 seasons. Member of the 1914 Boston Braves "Miracle" Team that won pennant, then World Series from Athletics in 4 games.

The listed statistics have long since been topped by other players. Perhaps they should have honored the other Maranville:

> Played more pranks than any other major league player. Funny-story total unsurpassed by anyone. Brought unlimited laughs to fans and teammates for 23 seasons. Member of that elite group of human beings who make the world a better place for their having been in it.

Walter James "Rabbit" Maranville

Born: November 11, 1891, Springfield, Massachusetts
Died: January 5, 1954, New York, New York
Height: 5'5", Weight: 155
Threw Right, Batted Right

YEAR	TEAM/L	G	AB	R	H	2B	3B	HR	RBI	BB	SO	AVG	SB
1911	New Bedford-NE	117	422	41	96	17	9	2	—	—	—	.227	—
1912	New Bedford-NE	122	452	65	128	22	4	4	—	—	—	.283	—
1912	Bos-N	26	86	8	18	2	0	0	8	9	14	.209	1
1913	Bos-N	143	571	68	141	13	8	2	48	68	62	.247	25
1914	Bos-N	156	586	74	144	23	6	4	78	45	56	.246	28
1915	Bos-N	149	509	51	124	23	6	2	43	45	65	.244	18
1916	Bos-N	155	604	79	142	16	13	4	38	50	69	.235	32
1917	Bos-N	142	561	69	146	19	13	3	43	40	47	.260	27
1918	Bos-N	11	38	3	12	0	1	0	3	4	0	.316	0
1919	Bos-N	131	480	44	128	18	10	5	43	36	23	.267	12
1920	Bos-N	134	493	48	131	19	15	1	43	28	24	.266	14
1921	Pit-N	153	612	90	180	25	12	1	70	47	38	.294	25
1922	Pit-N	155	672	115	198	26	15	0	63	61	43	.295	24
1923	Pit-N	141	581	78	161	19	9	1	41	42	34	.277	14
1924	Pit-N	152	594	62	158	33	20	2	71	35	53	.266	18
1925	Chi-N	75	266	37	62	10	3	0	23	29	20	.233	6
1926	Bro-N	78	234	32	55	8	5	0	24	26	24	.235	7
1927	StL-N	9	29	0	7	1	0	0	0	2	2	.241	0
1928	StL-N	112	366	40	88	14	10	1	34	36	27	.240	3
1929	Bos-N	146	560	87	159	26	10	0	55	47	33	.284	13
1930	Bos-N	142	558	85	157	26	8	2	43	48	23	.281	9
1931	Bos-N	145	562	69	146	22	5	0	33	56	34	.260	9
1932	Bos-N	149	571	67	134	20	4	0	37	46	28	.235	4
1933	Bos-N	143	478	46	104	15	4	0	38	36	34	.218	2
1935	Bos-N	23	67	3	10	2	0	0	5	3	3	.149	0
1936	Elmira-NYP	123	427	65	138	15	2	0	54	—	—	.323	—
1939	Albany-EL	6	17	3	2	0	0	0	2	—	—	.118	—
TOTAL ML		2670	10078	1255	2605	380	177	28	884	839	756	.258	291

World Series

YEAR	TEAM/L	G	AB	R	H	2B	3B	HR	RBI	BB	SO	AVG	SB
1914	Bos-N	4	13	1	4	0	0	0	3	1	1	.308	2
1928	StL-N	4	13	2	4	1	0	0	0	1	1	.308	1
TOTAL		8	26	3	8	1	0	0	3	2	2	.308	3

Index

Photo Credits

Dennis Goldstein 54, 68

John Holway 24

National Baseball Library 10, 18, 26, 36, 43, 44, 47, 50, 59, 76, 85, 89

Mark Rucker 66